MRS K.M. MATHEW'S
FINEST RECIPES

MRS K.M. MATHEW'S
FINEST RECIPES

EBURY
PRESS

An imprint of Penguin Random House

EBURY PRESS

USA | Canada | UK | Ireland | Australia
New Zealand | India | South Africa | China | Singapore

Ebury Press is part of the Penguin Random House group of companies
whose addresses can be found at global.penguinrandomhouse.com

Published by Penguin Random House India Pvt. Ltd
4th Floor, Capital Tower 1, MG Road,
Gurugram 122 002, Haryana, India

First published in India in Ebury Press by Penguin Random House India 2023

Cover and insert photos courtesy of Sumanth Kumar A.R.

10 9 8 7 6 5 4 3 2

The views and opinions expressed in this book are the author's own and the
facts are as reported by her which have been verified to the extent possible,
and the publishers are not in any way liable for the same.

ISBN 9780143453123

Typeset in Baskerville and Arima Madurai by Manipal Technologies Limited, Manipal
Printed at Replika Press Pvt. Ltd, India

www.penguin.co.in

This is a legitimate digitally printed version of the book and therefore might not
have certain extra finishing on the cover.

Contents

Foreword

My mother cradled two newborns in her arms in 1955. One was her last child (myself) and the other was her first book. It was a cookbook in Malayalam, titled *Pachaka Kala* (The Art of Cooking). Amma went on to write 23 more cookbooks, five of which were in English, over the next forty years. She also wrote three travelogues and a book on hair care, and edited the women's magazine *Vanitha* for 25 years. The book in your hands, *Mrs K.M. Mathew's Finest Recipes*, has been published 20 years after she left this world in 2003.

She left me more than a thousand recipes which she had collected, discovered or created. Amma had written her first cookery column on doughnuts, two years before I was born. It was published in the *Malayala Manorama* newspaper on 30 May 1953 along with her recipe for Goan Prawn Curry. These appeared under the name Mrs Annamma Mathew, and she became fairly well-known after a column on Mutton Bafath. Her popularity multiplied after she started using the name Mrs K.M. Mathew. This lucky name change was her own idea and she hardly ever used the name Annamma anywhere again.

It was my grandfather, K.C. Mammen Mappillai, who had spotted her talent while he was visiting my parents in Byculla, Bombay, and asked her to write a column in his newspaper. Fortunately, Amma was familiar with the varied tastes of India. Her parents were from Kerala, but she was born and brought up in faraway Kakinada, Andhra Pradesh, where her father was a doctor. He loved making chicken soup (he had made it even on the day he died, at the age of ninety-three) and her mother loved cooking Kerala's Syrian-Christian dishes. The neighbourhood was redolent with the scents of Tamil and Telugu food. Amma had always been partial to Tamil dishes, right from childhood till long after her college days in Madurai. It was later that she developed a love for Kannadiga delicacies in Chikmagalur, where my parents lived in a coffee estate in the first few years of their marriage. Then they moved to Bombay, and this was where she learnt to cook a variety of local, north Indian and continental dishes.

Amma had another advantage—she spoke fluent English, a gift not so common among Indian women in those days. This helped her enter the kitchens of even the most elite hotels, where she would never shy away from asking for recipes or other cooking advice from the chefs. Amma did it with natural grace, whether she was in India or travelling to other countries, in her forties. She was inspired to share the art of cooking for the sheer enjoyment of delicious food. She did not even recommend any complex or elaborate recipes to her readers because, for her, simplicity and taste came before novelty. She even avoided using words like 'foodie' and 'cuisine'. 'Simple good food' was her motto.

She wrote her recipes early in the morning, after waking up at 3 a.m. No recipe made it to her column before she had tested it at least three times. My father always got the first chance to taste it and to give feedback. Amma made sure she bought all the ingredients herself and measured them precisely. In the early years, she would use cigarette tins as measuring cups and gradually she accumulated all the paraphernalia, including a mallet from abroad for tenderizing the meat. When fair reviews of her books appeared in the press, she was ecstatic.

Food was sacred for Amma. She never wasted it. If there was anything left over, she would make a delicious new dish out of it. She always taught us to respect food and forbade shop talk at the dinner table at our home in Roopkala, Kottayam, Kerala. All she wanted was for everyone to enjoy good food. Far from secretive, she took joy in sharing her recipes with everyone. In fact, sometimes she would send the recipe along with the food she sent to her friends and acquaintances and if they ever faced a problem cooking it, she would even send her trained cook to demonstrate the cooking procedure.

Whoever visited Amma, she always gave out a packet of crisp savouries for them to take home. Her wedding gift to her acquaintances was invariably a bundle of her cookbooks. Even today, many people in India and abroad tell me that Amma's book *Nadan Pachakarama* was like the Bible to them when they had just started their married life and were learning to cook.

Even when she was in a wheelchair, in her twilight years, she remained engaged and active. When not cooking, she was often found reading books, appreciating art, singing songs, playing the violin, teaching music, raising funds for charity, guiding women's organizations, or supervising work at *Vanitha*. As a mother, she practised tough love, with a heart that remained tender inside. This book carries the essence of her soul.

Thangam Mammen

Snacks

1. Achappam
2. Kuzhalappam
3. Murukku
4. Chirotta
5. Kappa Bonda
6. Parippuvada
7. Karaboondi
8. Karasev
9. Pakkavada
10. Vatteyappam
11. Ethakka Appam
12. Jackfruit Elayappam
13. Unniyappam
14. Aval Vilayichathu
15. Avalos Unda
16. Groundnut Chikki
17. Sohan Laddu
18. Date Sweet
19. Black Halwa
20. White Halwa
21. Sharkarapuratti
22. Choux Pastry with Orient Filling
23. Coffee Cake
24. Citrus Cake with Milk Powder Icing
25. Rich Fruit Cake

1. Achappam

Sweet and crispy deep-fried cookies made with rice flour and coconut milk.

Yields: 30

INGREDIENTS

Raw rice: 3 cups

Water: 5 cups

Coconut milk: 2 cups

Eggs, whisked: 2

Sugar: 2 tsp

Salt to taste

Sesame seeds: 2 tsp

Cumin seeds: 1 tsp

Coconut oil or refined
vegetable oil for deep-frying

Achappam mould

METHOD

1. Soak the rice in water for 4 hours. Drain and transfer to a liquidizer.

2. Add coconut milk in small quantities alternating between the beaten eggs, sugar and salt, and grind to make a very thin batter. Pour this into a vessel. Add sesame seeds and cumin seeds.

3. Heat oil in a wok and dip the achappam mould in it.

4. Dip the hot mould in the batter ensuring not to immerse it completely.

5. Dip the mould coated with batter rapidly in hot oil. Lift the mould from oil after the cookie separates from it.

6. The achappam will float freely in the oil. Turn over and fry till golden brown on both sides. Drain off the excess oil and place the achappams on a kitchen tissue. Store in an airtight container.

Note: Excess sugar in the batter will make the achappam stick to the mould.

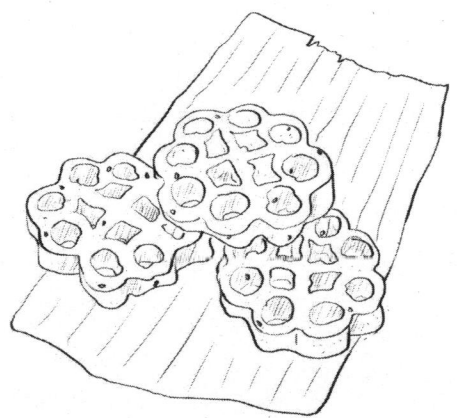

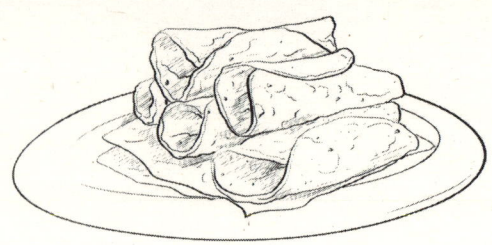

2. Kuzhalappam

A crunchy, savoury, anytime snack which is a favourite in central Kerala.

A modern twist to kuzhalappam is to serve it as a canape with meat filling or cheese with herbs.

Yields: 1 kg

INGREDIENTS

Raw rice: 4 cups

Coconut, finely grated: 2 cups

Cumin seeds: 1½ tsp

Shallots: 1¼ cups

Garlic cloves: 2

Salt to taste

Boiling water: 4 cups

Coconut oil or refined vegetable oil for frying

METHOD

1. Wash the rice 2 to 3 times and powder it as soon as the water is drained. Add 1 cup of grated coconut into the rice flour and mix lightly with your fingertips to free the mixture of any lumps. Set aside.

2. Extract ½ cup milk from the remaining 1 cup of grated coconut. Grind cumin seeds, shallots and garlic to a fine paste, and dissolve the ground paste and salt in the coconut milk.

3. Heat a heavy-bottomed vessel. Roast the coconut and rice flour mixture over a low flame for a few minutes, stirring constantly, until the moisture evaporates. Sprinkle the coconut milk and continue stirring till steam rises from the flour.

4. Reduce flame and add boiling water in batches. Keep stirring with a metal spatula. Remove from the flame and use hands to make a soft dough. Cover with a damp cloth and set aside for half an hour.

5. Divide the dough into small portions, the size of small lemons. Roll the dough into thin circles, on wax paper or greased banana leaves. Oil your index finger and wrap the rolled-out dough around it, pressing the overlapping edges together to form an elongated curl. Slide it off carefully keeping the shape intact and repeat till all the dough is used up. Deep fry, cool and store in airtight containers.

Note: The dough should be kneaded well for crisp kuzhalappams. When rolling out the dough, make batches, with each batch containing only as many curls as can be fried simultaneously.

3. Murukku

Though there are various types of murukkus and different recipes, this is among the best as it comes out light and crispy.

Yields: 800 g

INGREDIENTS

Split black beans
(Uzhunnu parippu): 1 cup

Husked green gram
(Cherupayar parippu): ½ cup

Water: 5 cups

Shallots: ½ cup

Garlic cloves: 5

Butter cut into small bits:
2 tbsp

Rice flour: 3 cups

Black sesame seeds: 3 tbsp

Cumin seeds: 1 tbsp

Asafoetida powder: 3 tsp

Salt to taste

Murukku press

Oil for deep-frying

METHOD

1. Pressure cook the black beans and green gram in 5 cups of water for 3 whistles. Keep the lid on till the steam escapes fully. Grind shallots and garlic to a paste.

2. In a bowl combine all the ingredients listed except oil. Mix well and knead into a tight soft dough.

3. Now divide the dough into approximately 6 small portions. Place one portion in a murukku press. Press the dough on to a lightly floured surface to form spiralling rounds.

4. With a greased spatula, gently lift each spiral and deep fry in batches in hot oil. Drain off excess oil, cool and store in airtight tins.

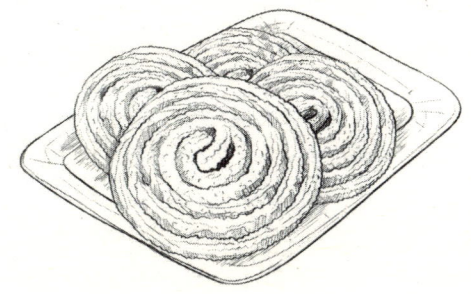

4. Chirotta

Good chirottas are light and flaky; they can be made spicy or sweet.

Yields: 60

INGREDIENTS

Rice flour: 4 tsp

Pepper powder: 1 tsp

Salt to taste

Flour: 3 cups

Warm oil: 2 tbsp

Salt: A pinch

Water to knead: 1 cup

Oil: 2 tsp

METHOD

1. Sieve rice flour, pepper powder and salt. Set aside. Mix flour, salt and oil and knead well with your fingertips until it resembles breadcrumbs. Add water a little at a time and make a tight but smooth dough.

2. Divide the dough into 8 balls and roll each ball into thin discs. Brush oil on top and bottom of the disc. Sprinkle rice flour mixture on top and bottom surfaces. Continue this process till the dough is used up.

3. Pile up the discs, one on top of the other, and roll them together. Set aside and cover with a damp kitchen towel to prevent it from drying.

4. With a sharp knife, slice this roll into quarter-inch circles. Now flatten each circle once more with a rolling pin into 2-inch diameter circles. Repeat the process with the rest of the dough.

5. Deep fry these in hot oil. Once cold, sprinkle pepper powder and store in airtight containers.

Note: The same recipe can be used to make sweet chirottas. Sprinkle powdered sugar instead of pepper powder.

5. Kappa Bonda

Bondas are a popular snack and make good starters too. Commonly made with potatoes,
the use of boiled tapioca (kappa) and a spicy filling makes for an interesting variation.

Yields: 30

INGREDIENTS

Kappa: 1 kg

Salt to taste

Eggs: 2

Breadcrumbs: 2 cups

For the filling

Coconut oil (optional): 1 tsp

Mustard seeds: ¼ tsp

Shallots, sliced: 15

Red chillies, broken: 8

Tamarind extract: ½ tsp

Salt to taste

METHOD

1. Cook the kappa in salt water. Mash it well to avoid any lumps.

2. Make small lemon-sized balls and keep aside.

3. For the filling, heat oil in a wok. Splutter mustard seeds, sauté the shallots and red chillies till the moisture evaporates. Add tamarind extract and salt to taste. Mix well.

4. Take each of the kappa balls and flatten a bit. Put a teaspoon of the filling in the centre and roll into a smooth ball.

5. Beat the eggs lightly. Dip the ball in the egg mixture. Roll in breadcrumbs.

6. Fry in oil and serve hot.

6. Parippuvada

A steaming cuppa and parippuvada is a great combination, served at tea shops all over southern India.
In Kerala, it is also eaten with small ripe bananas—the sweetness taking the edge off the spice.

Yields: 15

INGREDIENTS

Pigeon peas (tuvara parippu):
1 cup

Onion, finely chopped: ½ cup

Green chillies, chopped: 1 tsp

Ginger, finely chopped: 1 tsp

Curry leaves, finely chopped:
1 tbsp

Asafoetida powder: ½ tsp

Salt to taste

Coconut oil or refined
vegetable oil for frying

METHOD

1. Soak the pigeon peas in water for an hour. Drain and grind to a coarse paste.

2. Add the remaining ingredients and mix well.

3. Shape into rounds, each the size of a large lime.

4. Flatten slightly, and deep fry in hot oil till golden brown.

5. Drain and serve hot.

7. Karaboondi

The ubiquitous boondis, in this case kara (spicy), are a perfect complement
to ginger tea as a snack or mixed into yoghurt as 'boondi raita'.

Yields: 400 g

INGREDIENTS

Gram flour (besan) sifted:
½ kg

Baking soda: A pinch

Water: 2½ cups

Salt to taste

Chilli powder: ½ tsp

Curry leaves, fried: 2 sprigs

Roasted cashew nuts: 2 tbsp

Oil for frying

METHOD

1. Mix gram flour and water to make a loose batter. The water should be mixed carefully to avoid lumps forming in the batter.

2. Heat oil in a wok and pour the prepared batter into the hot oil through a slotted spoon; it will form small balls as it drops into the oil.

3. Drain when done and sprinkle chilli powder and salt. Add the fried curry leaves and cashew nuts.

4. Spread it out till it cools and store in airtight containers.

8. Karasev

An anytime munchie, this snack is best served with tea or coffee.

Yields: 400 g

INGREDIENTS

Gram flour: ½ kg

Water: 1 cup

Oil for frying: ¾ kg

Chilli powder: ½ tsp

Asafoetida: ½ tsp

Salt to taste

Idiyappam mould

METHOD

1. Mix gram flour and water and knead a dough similar to chapati dough.

2. Heat oil in a wok.

3. Put small quantities of the dough into the idiyappam mould and press the noodle-like strands into the hot oil. Fry till golden brown. Sprinkle salt, chilli and asafoetida powders and serve hot.

9. Pakkavada

This is also called ribbon pakkavada as its shape resembles bits of ribbon.

Yields: 500 g

INGREDIENTS

Gram flour (kadala maavu): 1 cup

Rice flour (appam powder): 1½ cups

Turmeric powder: ½ tsp

Chilli powder: 1 tbsp

Asafoetida powder: 1½ tsp

Fennel seed powder: 1 tsp

Garlic cloves: 7

Salt to taste

Butter: 1½ tbsp

Warm water

Curry leaves: A handful (optional)

Oil to fry

METHOD

1. Combine gram flour and rice flour.

2. Grind all the ingredients listed from turmeric powder to salt into a paste.

3. Mix butter with the ground paste and add these ingredients into the flour mixture. Work with your fingertips until the flour resembles breadcrumbs.

4. Sprinkle warm water, a little at a time, and knead till the dough is smooth.

5. Heat oil in a wok. Lightly fry the curry leaves and keep aside. Pass the dough through the press (sev mould) that has a ribbon mould. Fry it directly into the hot oil until brown. Mix fried curry leaves and serve.

10. Vatteyappam

A quintessential Kerala snack served during festivals and celebrations.

Wedges: 8

INGREDIENTS

Warm water: ½ cup

Sugar: 1 tsp

Yeast: 1 tbsp

Semolina: 2 tbsp

Water: 1½ cups

Fine rice flour: 2 cups

Coconut, grated and ground: 3 cups

Sugar: ¾ cup

Salt: A pinch

Cumin powder: 1 tsp

Cardamom powder: ½ tsp

Raisins: 12

METHOD

1. Dissolve 1 tsp sugar in warm water and sprinkle yeast. Allow to froth.

2. In a pan, mix semolina and water. Cook to make a gruel. Set aside to cool.

3. Grind coconut with sugar. Set aside.

4. Mix and knead rice flour, yeast, gruel, ground coconut with sugar and salt to make a thick batter. Set aside to ferment for 1 hour.

5. Mix the cumin and cardamom powders before pouring the batter.

6. Pour into an 8-inch greased mould. Scatter raisins on top. Steam for 25 minutes in a pressure cooker without placing the weight or cook in a steamer. Cut into wedges like slices of cake and serve. Alternately this can be steamed in idli moulds.

11. Ethakka Appam

Ripe plantain slices dipped in batter and deep fried to perfection; this remains a favourite in Kerala.

Yields: 36

INGREDIENTS

Ripe bananas, peeled: 6

Water: ½ cup

Rice flour: ½ cup

Flour: 1 cup

Sugar: 1 tsp

Baking soda: A pinch

Salt: A pinch

Oil for frying

METHOD

1. Slice each banana in half, lengthwise and cut each slice in half, again.

2. Make a thick batter of rice flour, flour and water. Add sugar, baking soda and salt.

3. Dip the banana slices in the batter and deep fry in hot oil until golden brown.

4. Drain off excess oil by placing on paper towels. Serve hot.

12. Jackfruit Elayappam

A soft, thin pancake with jackfruit, jaggery and coconut filling.

Yields: 8

INGREDIENTS

Jackfruit preserve: 2 cups

Water: 2¼ cups

Vegetable oil: 2 tsp

Salt to taste

Rice flour: 2 cups

Banana leaves cut into 8 portions

METHOD

1. Boil 2 cups of water with oil and salt. Reduce the flame and gradually add flour while stirring.

2. Remove from the flame and knead into a smooth dough. Divide the dough into 8 portions.

3. Dissolve sugar in ¼ cup water. Add the grated coconut and cook over a low flame till all the water is absorbed. Remove from the flame and add the jackfruit preserve. Mix well. Divide the mixture into 8 portions.

4. Clean and wipe the banana leaves dry. Spread a portion of the dough evenly on each leaf using your fingertips. It should be spread thin.

5. Spread a portion of the jackfruit preserve evenly over one half of the dough. Fold over the other half. Press and seal the sides. Repeat till the dough and filling are used up.

6. Steam the elayappams for 30 minutes.

Jackfruit Preserve

Yields: 4 kg

INGREDIENTS

Ripe jackfruit mashed in a mixer: 4 kg

Jaggery: 1 kg

Water: 4 cups

Ghee: 200 g

Cardamom powder: 2 heaped tsp

METHOD

1. Dissolve jaggery in water. Strain into a heavy-bottomed vessel and cook over a low flame to make into a thick syrup.

2. Add the mashed jackfruit into the jaggery syrup. Stir well. As it thickens, keep adding ghee, a little at a time. Mix well, remove from fire and add cardamom powder.

13. Unniyappam

These sweet round fritters are a favourite snack made with rice, jaggery and mashed bananas;
served at festivals and special occasions.

Yields: 15

INGREDIENTS

Jaggery, grated: 100 g

Water: 1 cup

Fine rice flour: 1 cup

Coconut, finely chopped and
fried in ghee: ½ cup

Ripe bananas, mashed: ½ cup

Sugar: 1 tbsp

Baking soda: ⅛ tsp

METHOD

1. Melt jaggery in 1 cup water and cook to make a thick syrup. Transfer the rest of the ingredients to a bowl and add the melted jaggery. Mix well and make a batter of dropping consistency.

2. Drop a spoonful of the batter into hot oil and deep fry till golden brown. If an unniyappam chatti (pan) is available, pour spoonfuls of batter into the oiled moulds, turning over until both sides are golden brown.

14. Aval Vilayichathu

Another typical central Kerala snack, this is traditionally served with small bananas.

Yields: 1½ kg (Serves 40)

INGREDIENTS

Ghee: ½ cup

Coconut slivers: 1½ cups

Black sesame seeds: ½ cup

Roasted gram: ¼ cup

Jaggery: 1½ kg

Water: 6 cups

Coconuts, finely grated: 4

Beaten rice: ½ kg

Cardamom powder: 2 tsp

METHOD

1. Heat the ghee in a pan. Lightly fry together the coconut slivers, black sesame seeds and roasted gram. Set aside.

2. Dissolve the jaggery in 6 cups water. Strain into a heavy-bottomed vessel and heat again. Switch off the flame before it boils. Let it cool slightly. Add grated coconut, beaten rice and cardamom powder. Mix well.

3. Lastly, add the fried ingredients and serve.

15. Avalos Unda

A popular dish in Syrian-Christian homes, this requires adeptness and experience to get the right consistency.

Yields: 40

INGREDIENTS

Sugar: ¼ kg

Water: ½ cup

Lime juice: 1 tbsp

Melted ghee: ½ tbsp

Avalos powder: ½ kg

Cardamom powder: ½ tsp

For avalos powder

Rice: 1 kg

Grated coconut: ½ kg

Cumin seeds: 1 tsp

Salt to taste

METHOD

1. Soak 1 kg rice in water for 2 hours. Drain the water and powder the slightly damp rice. Sieve the flour and mix in grated coconut with fingertips. Add cumin seeds and salt to taste. Mix well. Compact the mixture in a bowl to retain moisture and set aside for 2 hours.

2. Roast this mixture in a heavy skillet over high flame until golden brown. Cool and sieve to remove any lumps.

3. Powder the lumps and roast again and add to the prepared avalos powder. Cool and store in airtight containers.

To make the undas (balls)

1. In a bowl, mix the avalos powder and cardamom powder. Set aside. Keep aside 5 tbsp of avalos powder to roll the undas.

2. Mix sugar, water and lime juice. Keep on fire and cook to one-thread consistency. Add ghee and remove from flame. Cool slightly and add the syrup to the avalos powder. Mix well and shape into small balls, the size of limes.

3. Toss the balls lightly in avalos powder and store in an airtight tin.

16. Groundnut Chikki

Delicious sticky bars that are an addictive treat and quite easy to make in your own kitchen.

Yields: 12

INGREDIENTS

Groundnuts, roasted: 1 cup

Sugar: ½ cup

Butter: ¼ tsp

Baking soda: ¼ tsp

METHOD

1. Crumble groundnuts.

2. Brown the sugar in a heavy skillet and add butter.

3. Add baking soda. When the mixture begins to froth, add the crumbled groundnuts. Remove from flame and mix well.

4. Pour into a greased tray or on to a marble slab and level the surface with a rolling pin.

5. Cut into desired shapes before the mixture hardens. Store in airtight containers.

Note: Prolonged exposure to air will make the chikki soggy.

17. Sohan Laddu

Laddus made with wheat flour, a tasty variation.

Yields: 40

INGREDIENTS

Ghee: 2 tbsp

Cashew nuts, finely chopped:
2 tbsp

Wheat flour: 3 cups

Cardamom powder: 2 tsp

Powdered sugar: 1 cup

Ghee: 1¾ cup

Sugar: ¼ cup

METHOD

1. In a wok, fry the cashew nuts in 1 tbsp ghee and keep aside.

2. Add wheat flour to the same wok and sauté mildly. Remove from flame.

3. When cool, add powdered sugar. Mix well and keep aside.

4. Melt ¼ cup sugar and pour on a greased metal tray. When cool, remove and crush into small pieces.

5. Mix the rest of the melted ghee, fried cashew nuts and crushed sugar pieces with the flour.

6. When the mixture is warm, make lime-sized balls and store in airtight containers.

18. Date Sweet

Cashews and cornflakes give these special sweet balls a tasty crunch.

Yields: 12

INGREDIENTS

Dates, chopped: 1 cup

Butter: ½ cup

Sugar: ½ cup

Cashew nuts, broken: ½ cup

Egg, beaten: 1

Vanilla essence: 1 tsp

Desiccated coconut: 1½ cups

Cornflakes, crushed: 2 cups

METHOD

1. In a bowl, beat the butter. Add dates, beaten egg, cashew nuts, sugar and vanilla essence and mix well. Transfer all the ingredients to a pan. Cook on low flame.

2. When the sugar begins to melt, remove from flame.

3. When cool, mix with cornflakes, make balls and roll in the desiccated coconut.

19. Black Halwa

Jaggery and coconut milk give this halwa a distinct and irresistible taste,
very different from the popular Kozhikkodan (north Kerala) halwa.

Yields: 2½ kg

INGREDIENTS

Water: 6 cups

Flour: ½ kg

Jaggery: 1¾ kg

Coconut milk from 3
coconuts: 12 cups

Ghee: 1½ cups

Sugar: ½ cup

Cardamom powder: 1 tbsp

Cashew nut slivers: 2 cups

METHOD

1. Knead the flour well using 2 cups of water to make a soft dough.

2. Reserve 3 cups water and add the remaining water a little at a time to the dough to make a thin batter.

3. Strain the batter through a muslin cloth to remove any lumps. Set aside for an hour and decant the clean liquid from the top.

4. Melt the jaggery in 6 cups water and strain the syrup. Mix the batter, jaggery syrup and coconut milk together in a heavy vessel. The consistency should be that of milk.

5. Bring to a boil, stirring constantly till quite thick. Stir in the ghee in small quantities, stirring all the time till the mixture forms into a soft ball.

6. Add sugar, cardamom powder and half of the cashew nut slivers.

7. Cook over low flame till the ghee separates.

8. Remove from flame and pour into a greased tray. Sprinkle the remaining cashew nut slivers on top and smooth the surface.

Note: While making the halwa, start on a high flame, then gradually reduce the heat as the cooking progresses. The halwa should be cooked slowly for 2 hours.

20. White Halwa

Milk and sugar replace coconut milk and jaggery in this recipe.

Yields: 2½ kg

INGREDIENTS

Water: 6 l

Flour: ½ kg

Sugar: 1½ kg

Milk: 2 l

Ghee: 1½ cups

Sugar: ½ cup

Cardamom powder: 1 tbsp

Cashew nut slivers: 2 cups

Lime juice: 1 tbsp

METHOD

1. Knead the flour to make a soft dough using 2 cups water.

2. Reserve 3 cups water and add the remaining water a little at a time to the dough to make a thin batter. Strain the batter through a muslin cloth to remove any lumps. Set aside for 1 hour and decant clear liquid from the top.

3. Dissolve 1½ kg sugar in 3 cups water. Strain and set aside. Mix the batter, sugar syrup and milk in a heavy vessel. Bring to a boil, stirring continuously.

4. As it thickens, add the ghee, stirring continuously. Cook over a low flame till the ghee separates.

5. Add ½ cup sugar and 1 tbsp lime juice. Stir well till it starts leaving the sides of the vessel. Add cardamom powder and half of the cashew nut slivers. Transfer to a greased plate and spread evenly. Scatter the remaining cashew nut slivers on top.

Note: While making the halwa, start on a high flame, then gradually lower the heat as the cooking progresses. The halwa should be cooked slowly for 2 hours.

21. Sharkarapuratti

Sharkarapuratti has an important place on the sadya (traditional feast) leaf, though it is also a popular snack.

Yields: 600 g

INGREDIENTS

Raw bananas: ½ kg

Vegetable oil for frying: 2 cups

Jaggery: ¼ kg

Cumin powder: ½ tsp

Dried ginger powder: ½ tsp

Rice flour: 2 tsp

Sugar: 1 tsp

METHOD

1. Pare the bananas, wash and dry well. Slice into round sections of even thickness, about ¼ inch, and then cut into quarters.

2. Deep fry the slices in hot oil till crisp. Sprinkle a little salt water in the oil. Stir so that the salt is evenly absorbed by the chips. When the spluttering subsides, remove the chips from the oil, place in a strainer and let the oil drain.

3. Dissolve jaggery in water. Strain and heat to make a syrup of one-thread consistency. Lower the flame and stir the banana chips into the syrup. Mix well to coat the chips uniformly with the syrup.

4. Sprinkle cumin and dried ginger powders. Stir well, taking care not to break the chips.

5. Remove from fire and sprinkle a mixture of rice flour and sugar. Stir till separated, cool and store in airtight containers.

Note: Use only mature but unripe bananas to make the chips.

22. Choux Pastry with Orient Filling

A favourite with young people, the trick here is to master the art of making choux pastry.

Yields: 10

INGREDIENTS

For the filling

Chicken, cooked and shredded: 1 cup

Pepper: 1 tsp

Salt to taste

Chicken stock: ½ cup

Oil: ¼ cup

Cornflour: ½ tsp

Onion, chopped: 1 cup

Garlic, minced: 1 tbsp

Ginger, minced: 1 tsp

Green capsicum, chopped: ½ cup

Celery, minced: A handful

Soy sauce: ½ tbsp

For choux pastry

Flour: 1 cup

Salt: A pinch

Water: 1 cup

Butter: ½ cup

Eggs: 4

METHOD

1. Cook the chicken with salt, pepper and soy sauce. Reserve ½ cup of stock. Dice chicken into small pieces.

2. Heat oil in a wok and sauté the onions until transparent, and add the ginger and garlic. Add the chicken, capsicum and celery and sauté again. Keep the sautéed ingredients to one side, add cornflour and stir till it becomes slightly brown. Pour the stock and mix all the ingredients together until it thickens.

METHOD

1. Preheat the oven to 375°F.

2. Heat a pan and boil water with a pinch of salt. As the water starts boiling, add butter followed by flour. Keep stirring till the water is absorbed and a dough is formed. Remove from heat. Break the eggs and blend well into the dough, using a wooden spatula.

3. Grease a baking tray. Pour a teaspoonful of this dough on the tray. You can also use a piping bag with a big nozzle, and pipe equal size portions of the dough on the tray. Lightly brush the tops with beaten egg and bake in the preheated oven. Once the pastry puffs up and starts getting brown, remove from oven and let it cool.

4. Slit a small portion of the choux pastry and fill one teaspoon of the filling. Serve.

Note: The choux pastry can also be filled with a sweet filling.

23. Coffee Cake

A soft and moist cake; the icing lends a special touch.

Yields: 24 slices

INGREDIENTS

Flour: 200 g

Baking powder: ½ tsp

Baking soda: ¼ tsp

Butter: 250 g

Powdered sugar: 250 g

Egg yolks: 4

Thick coffee (cold), prepared with 3 tsp of coffee powder and 2 tbsp of hot water

Egg whites: 4

Vanilla essence: 1 tsp

Orange juice: 2 tbsp

Orange rind, ground: ½ tsp

Cashew nuts, finely chopped, fried in ghee: ¼ cup

For the icing

Cocoa powder: 1 tbsp

Instant coffee powder: 1 tsp

Water: ¼ cup

Sugar: 250 g

Water: ¾ cup

Egg white: 1

Salt: A pinch

Chopped nuts: 1 cup

METHOD

1. Sieve flour, baking powder and baking soda.

2. Whip together butter, sugar, egg yolks and coffee solution into a soft fluffy mixture.

3. Whisk the egg whites. Add vanilla essence and ground orange rind and whisk again.

4. Set the oven to 350°F.

5. Mix the creamed butter and flour mixture. Add orange juice and cashew nuts. Fold in the egg whites and bake in the preheated oven for 40 minutes.

6. Mix cocoa and coffee powders. Dissolve in water and cook to make a thick cream. Remove and cool.

7. Make a one-string syrup with the sugar and water in an oil-free skillet. Whisk the egg white until stiff.

8. Add salt. Pour the sugar syrup into the egg white and beat with a fork. When it becomes like butter, add the cocoa-coffee cream and mix well. Spread this cream mixture over the cake. Sprinkle nuts on top and lightly press them on to the surface before the cream sets.

24. Citrus Cake with Milk Powder Icing

Lemon or orange gives cakes a burst of freshness and this recipe is a treat with its unique icing.

Yields: 15 slices

INGREDIENTS

Flour: 2¼ cups

Baking powder: ¾ tsp

Baking soda: ¼ tsp

Butter: 1½ cups

Powdered sugar: 2 cups

Egg yolks: 3

Lime rind, grated: 1 tsp

Lime juice: 2 tbsp

Lukewarm milk: ½ cup

Egg whites: 4

Sugar: 4 tbsp

Vanilla essence: ½ tsp

METHOD

1. Set the oven to 350°F. Sift flour, baking powder and baking soda together.

2. Cream butter and sugar until soft and fluffy. Add egg yolks one by one and beat well. Add lemon rind and juice. Beat again. Fold in the sifted flour and milk alternately mixing gently with a spoon.

3. Whisk the egg whites stiff. Sprinkle sugar, a little at a time, and continue beating till sugar is over. Add vanilla essence. Fold the egg whites into the cake batter.

4. Line a cake tin with greased paper and pour in the batter. Bake in the preheated oven for 30 minutes or until a tester comes out clean.

5. Remove from oven and leave in the cake pan for 10 minutes. Then place on a wire rack to cool. Ice with milk powder icing.

Milk Powder Icing

INGREDIENTS

Sugar: ½ cup

Water: 1 cup

Icing sugar: 300 g

Butter: 2 tbsp

Milk powder: 1 cup

Vanilla essence: ½ tsp

Baking powder: 2 pinches

METHOD

1. Place a pan on low heat. Add sugar and water. Cook until the sugar is dissolved. Add the icing sugar and mix well. Continue stirring to prevent any lumps and remove from flame. Beat the butter. Add the milk powder and continue beating. Sprinkle baking powder and vanilla essence and beat again.

2. Pour this icing evenly on the cake. With a palette knife, cover all uneven surfaces.

3. Food colouring can be added according to your choice.

25. Rich Fruit Cake

A speciality of the Christmas season, this cake is rich and redolent with myriad flavours and is everyone's favourite.

Yields: 1½ kg

INGREDIENTS

Eggs: 4

Butter: Weight of eggs

Castor sugar: Weight of eggs

Flour: Weight of eggs + ½ cup flour to coat the fruits and nuts

Baking powder: 1 tsp

Salt: 1 level tsp

Cinnamon powder: ½ tsp

Cloves, powdered: ½ tsp

Cardamom powder: ½ tsp

Nutmeg powder: ¼ tsp

Cocoa powder: 1 tbsp

Instant coffee powder: 1 tsp

Water: 2 tbsp

Candied mixed peel and ginger: ½ cup

Currants or black sultanas: ½ cup

Raisins: 1 cup

Dates, seedless: ½ cup

Cherries: ½ cup

Cashew nuts: ½ cup

Brandy: 1 cup

Vanilla essence: 1 tsp

METHOD

1. Prepare the fruits 3 days in advance. Clean and chop the fruits and nuts. Soak them in 1 cup of brandy and keep it for 3 days in an airtight jar. The day you bake the cake, coat the soaked fruits and nuts with ½ cup of flour. Set aside.

2. Preheat the oven to 320°F. Line the baking tins with greased paper.

3. Sift the flour with baking powder and spices.

4. Cream the butter and sugar. Add eggs one by one and continue beating till it is light and fluffy.

5. Mix cocoa and coffee powders in water. Add this to the caramel syrup along with the essences and jams. Add these ingredients to the creamed mixture. Finally, fold the sieved flour into this mixture. Lastly, add the fruits and nuts, and mix well.

Almond essence: A drop

Honey: 2 tbsp

Pineapple jam: 2 tbsp

Orange marmalade: 2 tbsp

Caramel syrup: made from
caramelizing 1½ cups sugar
cooked with 1 cup hot water

6. Spoon this mixture into the prepared cake tins, filling them halfway.

7. Bake the cake in a slow oven at 300°F for 15 minutes, and then reduce the temperature to 275°F and bake for another 45 minutes. Check with a tester to see if the cake is done.

Breakfast Items

1. Palappam
2. Vegetable Stew
3. Vellayappam
4. Idiyappam
5. Puttu
6. Black Chickpea Curry
7. Ney Pathiri
8. Pathiri
9. Uppumav
10. Parottas

1. Palappam

A staple in central Kerala, and now popular in south Indian restaurants everywhere,
this is made in a special wok called the appachatti or an appam pan.

Yields: 20

INGREDIENTS

Water: 1½ cups

Sugar: 2 tbsp

Semolina: 2 tbsp

Yeast: 1 tsp

Rice flour: 2 cups

Coconut milk: 2 cups

Salt to taste

Appam pan

Gingelly oil

METHOD

1. Mix water, semolina and sugar in a pan. Cook to make a gruel. When the gruel turns lukewarm, add yeast and allow it to froth up. Add rice flour and mix well to make a loose dough. Keep the dough covered for 1 hour to rise. Add coconut milk and salt to taste. Make a thick batter.

2. Heat an appam pan on low flame. Lightly brush the surface with gingelly oil.

3. Pour in a ladleful of the batter, lift the pan and swirl rapidly once. The batter should coat the edges of the pan to form a lacy border and the rest of the batter should settle in the centre. Cover the pan with a lid. Cook for 4 to 5 minutes until the centre is cooked well and the sides are golden. Remove gently with a spatula.

4. Repeat till all the batter is used up. Serve with vegetable or chicken stew.

2. Vegetable Stew

This is traditionally served with appams.

Serves: 10

INGREDIENTS

Oil: ½ cup

Cardamoms: 2

Cloves: 3

Cinnamon: 1 inch

Star anise: 1

Pepper powder: ½ tsp

Turmeric powder: ½ tsp

Onions, sliced: 2

Green chillies, split: 4

Ginger, sliced: 1-inch piece

Garlic cloves, sliced: 6

Tomato, cut in wedges: 1

Salt to taste

Cauliflower florets: 1 cup

Carrot: Cut into 1-inch cubes

Peas: ½ cup

Potato, medium-sized: Cut into 1-inch cubes

Shredded coconut for thick milk: 1 cup

Thin milk: 3 cups

Ghee: 2 tbsp

Shallots, sliced: 5

Curry leaves: 1 sprig

METHOD

1. Heat oil and sauté the cardamom, cloves, cinnamon and star anise.

2. Add the sliced onion, chillies, ginger and garlic. Once the onions are transparent, add turmeric and pepper powders.

3. Mix in the vegetables and sauté well. Add thin milk, salt to taste and let the vegetables cook.

4. Finally, add the tomatoes.

5. Pour in the thick milk and when it starts to boil, remove from flame.

6. In a small pan, heat ghee. Add shallots and curry leaves. Fry until the shallots are brown. Pour the tempering over the stew.

3. Vellayappam

Resembling an American pancake, vellayappams are slightly sweet and fermented using yeast. Fresh, sweet toddy was used for fermentation back in the day but now yeast is a more commonly used alternative.

Yields: 15

INGREDIENTS

Water: 1 cup

Sugar: 2 tbsp

Semolina: 2 tbsp

Lukewarm water: 1 cup

Sugar: ½ tsp

Yeast: ½ tsp

Coconut, grated: 1

Shallots: 6

Cumin seeds: 1 tsp

Rice flour: 2 cups

Water: Enough to make a thick batter

Salt: ½ tsp

METHOD

1. In a pan, cook semolina and sugar with 1 cup water to make a gruel. Set this aside to cool.

2. Dissolve ½ tsp sugar in 1 cup lukewarm water and add yeast. Allow it to ferment for 10 minutes.

3. Grind the grated coconut with shallots and cumin seeds to form a smooth paste. Mix the rice flour, gruel, yeast and coconut paste. Knead well.

4. Add sufficient water to make a thick batter, almost like a pancake or an idli batter. Keep aside for 2 hours and allow to rise.

5. Add salt to taste and mix well. Allow the batter to rise again.

6. Pour a ladleful of batter on a greased iron skillet and spread like a thick pancake. Small bubbles will appear on the surface of the appam. Cover and cook on low flame.

7. After a couple of minutes, turn it over and cook until it turns slightly brown. Remove from flame.

8. These appams can be served with vegetable or meat stew.

4. Idiyappam

These hoppers are best enjoyed with curry or sweetened coconut milk.

Yields: 18

INGREDIENTS

Water: 1½ cups

Vegetable oil: 1 tbsp

Salt to taste

Rice flour, roasted: 3 cups

Coconut, grated: 1 cup

Idli moulds

METHOD

1. Boil a pan of water with salt and oil. Remove from flame.

2. Slowly pour the hot water into rice flour, stirring all the time to prevent lumps.

3. When cool enough to handle, knead well to form a soft dough.

4. Divide the dough into small portions and squeeze each portion through a press (idiyappam achu) directly into the idli moulds. Top with grated coconut and steam for 7 to 10 minutes.

5. Serve hot with sweetened coconut milk, meat or vegetable stew.

5. Puttu

Puttu or steamed funnel rice cakes (shapes can vary) can be paired with a variety of savoury and sweet accompaniments. Puttu can also be made with wheat or ragi flour.

Yields: 2

INGREDIENTS

Rice flour, slightly coarse: 2 cups

Water: As required

Salt to taste

Puttu maker

METHOD

1. Add salt to the flour. Sprinkle water over the flour and mix lightly to form a dry mixture like breadcrumbs. Make sure lumps do not form.

2. Line the puttu maker with grated coconut, followed by rice flour. Do this alternately until the puttu maker is full. Make sure you end with grated coconut.

3. Now, steam the puttu for 5 minutes. Remove from flame.

4. Repeat the process till the mixture is used up. Serve hot.

6. Black Chickpea Curry

Serves: 4

INGREDIENTS

Oil: 3 tbsp

Kadala (black chickpea): 1 cup

Cardamom: 1

Cinnamon: 1 piece

Water: 2½ cups

Coconut bits: 3 tbsp

Soda powder: 1 pinch

Salt to taste

Onions, sliced: 2

Ginger, julienned: 1 piece

Garlic cloves: 6

Bay leaf: 1

Coriander powder: 1 tbsp

Chilli powder: 1 tsp

Turmeric powder: ½ tsp

Garam masala: 1 tsp

Soy sauce: 1 tbsp

Mustard seeds: ½ tsp

Curry leaves

Oil: 2 tbsp

METHOD

1. Soak black chickpeas in water for 5 hours. Transfer to a pressure cooker. Add cardamom, cinnamon, coconut bits, soda powder and salt and cook for 5 whistles.

2. Heat oil in a wok. Add sliced onions, ginger, garlic and bay leaf and sauté well. Add coriander, chilli and turmeric powders and garam masala and sauté until the oil separates. Mix in soy sauce and sauté again. Add the cooked chickpeas with its stock. Once it boils, lower the flame. Close the wok with a lid and let the curry simmer for 10 minutes. Check salt and add if required. Remove from the flame.

3. Heat oil in a pan. Add mustard seeds and let it splutter. Add curry leaves. Lightly fry and pour over the curry.

7. Ney Pathiri

More common in north Kerala, this delicacy is made especially for Iftar, during the month of Ramzan.

Yields: 20

INGREDIENTS

Rice flour: 1 cup

American flour (maida): 1 cup

Shredded coconut: 1 cup

Aniseed: ½ tbsp

Cumin seeds: ½ tbsp

Black sesame seeds: ¼ tsp

Boiling water: 1½ cups

Ghee: 1 tbsp

Salt to taste

Oil for frying

METHOD

1. Sieve the rice flour and flour. Mix with coconut, aniseed, cumin seeds and black sesame seeds. Set aside.

2. Boil water, salt and ghee (ney) and add to the sieved ingredients little by little. Mix well and keep stirring till a soft dough is formed. Make small lime-sized balls and flatten each ball into circular rounds and roll out like a poori.

3. Heat some oil in a small wok and deep fry the rounds until they are golden brown. Serve hot with any curry.

8. Pathiri

The pathiri goes well with chicken or meat curry. It can also be soaked in coconut milk for another layer of flavour.

Yields: 6

INGREDIENTS

Rice flour: 1 cup

Thick coconut milk: ½ cup

Salt to taste

Vegetable oil: ½ tsp

Water: 1½ cups

METHOD

1. Add salt and oil to water and boil in a closed vessel.

2. Lower the flame and add the flour, stirring well to prevent lumps from forming. Cook over a low flame till all the water is absorbed. Remove from the flame and when cool enough to handle, knead well to make a soft dough, without adding any water.

3. Divide the dough into 1-inch balls, sprinkle rice flour and roll them out into very thin circles. Trim the edges with a round cutter. Place the pathiri on a heated cast-iron griddle.

4. Turn it over after a few seconds and cook till it puffs up.

5. Remove from flame and spoon over some coconut milk.

Note: Best with mutton, chicken or vegetable stew.

9. Uppumav

A favourite breakfast dish all over the South, this can be prepared in just a few minutes.
Add some ghee while hot to add flavour and softness.

Serves: 6

INGREDIENTS

Ghee: ¼ cup

Split urad dal: 2 tsp

Dry red chillies, split
into two: 2

Green chilli, finely chopped:
½ tbsp

Ginger, finely chopped: ½ tbsp

Sprig of curry leaves,
chopped: 1 tbsp

Semolina: 2 cups

Water: 6 cups

Salt: ½ tsp

Cashew nuts, fried and
broken: 2 tbsp

Coriander leaves: A few

Mustard seeds: ½ tsp

Onion: ¾ cup

Butter: 1 tsp

METHOD

1. Heat ghee in a wok, and splutter mustard seeds and split urad dal. Add onions, cashew nuts, red chillies, green chilli, ginger and curry leaves. Sauté these ingredients.

2. Add semolina and keep stirring till it is roasted well. Once this is done, add 6 cups of boiling water all at once over the sautéed ingredients. Add salt. Bring it to a boil. Stir continuously, allowing the water to be absorbed. Add butter and stir again till the spoon comes out clean.

3. Remove from the flame. Garnish with coriander leaves. Serve warm.

10. Parottas

The secret to soft and flaky parottas lies in the softness of the dough and the layering process.

Yields: 15

INGREDIENTS

Flour: ½ kg

Egg: 1

Sugar: 1 tsp

Curd (not too sour): 1 tbsp

Milk: As required to make a soft dough (¼ cup approx.)

Salt to taste

Vegetable fat or ghee

METHOD

1. Mix all the ingredients except oil and make a loose dough. Punch and knead the dough several times until it is soft and smooth. Cover with a wet cloth and set aside for 4 hours.

2. Knead again before making the parotta. Roll the dough into a log. Break a portion of the log and shape it into a lime-sized ball. Roll it out round and thin on a floured board. Spread warm ghee or fat on it, pleat lengthwise from one end to the other and twist each pleat into a round.

3. Flatten it again with your hand or roll it gently without applying pressure. Cook on a hot greased iron griddle till both sides are well done.

4. Pile up three or four parottas together and compress between your palms. This will help separate the layers.

Note: You can use water instead of milk while kneading the dough, but milk will make softer parottas.

Egg Dishes

1. Egg Roast

Onions sautéed with spices and tomatoes make this a special dish that goes well with appams and even chapatis.

Serves: 4

INGREDIENTS

Eggs: 4

Chilli powder: 1 tsp

Coriander powder: 1 tsp

Pepper powder: ½ tsp

Aniseed: ½ tsp

Cinnamon: 1

Cloves: 2

Cardamom pod: 1

Oil: 3 tbsp

Onions, chopped: 1 cup

Tomatoes, chopped: ¼ cup

Water: ¼ cup

Salt to taste

METHOD

1. Hard-boil and shell the eggs. Keep them aside.

2. Grind chilli, coriander, pepper powders, aniseed and all the spices.

3. Heat oil in a wok and fry the onions until transparent. Add the ground paste and fry on a low flame until the oil surfaces. Stir in the tomatoes and continue frying on low heat. After the tomatoes are blended well, add salt and ¼ cup water. Cover the pan and simmer till the gravy is thick.

4. Halve the eggs and arrange on a serving dish. Pour the gravy over. Serve hot.

2. Egg Curry

The coconut milk gravy with boiled eggs and soft chunky potatoes makes
this a great side dish for appams, idiyappams and parottas.

Serves: 6

INGREDIENTS

Eggs, hard-boiled: 6

Potato, cut into quarters: 1

Oil: 2 tbsp

Onion, finely sliced: 1 cup

Green chillies, slit into half: 3

Ginger, sliced: 1 tsp

Garlic cloves, sliced: 4

Curry leaves: 2

Tomato, chopped: 1

Coriander powder: 1 tbsp

Turmeric powder: ½ tsp

Spice powder: 1 tsp

Salt to taste

Coconut, grated: 2 cups (for extracting milk)

1st extract of coconut milk: 1 cup

2nd extract of coconut milk: 1 cup

For the spice powder

Aniseed: 1 cup

Cumin seeds: 3 tbsp

Cardamom seeds: 36

Cloves: 36

Cinnamon, 1-inch pcs: 18

Star anise: 3

Nutmeg: 3

Mace: 3

METHOD

1. Hard-boil and shell the eggs.

2. Heat the oil and sauté the onion, green chillies, ginger, garlic and curry leaves. Add the tomatoes and sauté well.

3. Make a paste of coriander, turmeric and spice powders with a little water. Add this paste to the sautéed ingredients and fry well.

4. Cut the potato into quarters and mix with the sautéed ingredients. Add salt to taste. Pour the thin coconut milk. Cook till potatoes are soft.

5. Finally, stir in the thick coconut milk and mix well. Halve the eggs and add to the gravy. Remove from the flame and serve.

METHOD

For the spice powder

1. Heat a skillet and add all the ingredients. Roast them on medium flame and when done, cool completely. Transfer to a mixer jar and powder finely. Store in airtight jars.

Meat Dishes

1. Kerala Meat Fry with Coconut Bits
2. Meat Stew
3. Meat Pattichu Varathathu
4. Mutton Chops
5. Mutton Piralen
6. Mutton Chilli Fry
7. Mutton Bafath
8. Mutton Red Curry
9. Mutton Kurma
10. Meatball Curry
11. Roasted Raan
12. Veal Roast
13. Veal Chops
14. Roast Beef
15. Beef Chops
16. Beef Steak
17. Masala Cutlet
18. Kola Balls with Mint and Raisin Chutney
19. Mutton Liver Fry
20. Pork Vindaloo
21. Chicken Curry Country Style
22. Trivandrum Chicken
23. Masala Chicken
24. Ellu Chicken
25. Pepper Chicken
26. Chicken Piralen
27. Murgh Masala
28. Murgh Mughlai
29. New Year Chicken Roast
30. Chicken Roast with Sauces
31. Easter Chicken Roast
32. Chicken Roast with Pomegranate Seeds
33. Chicken with Puttu
34. Simple Chicken Roast
35. Minced Meat-Stuffed Brinjal
36. Mixed Meat Grill
37. Kuttanad Duck Curry
38. Duck Fry with Gravy
39. Special Duck Curry
40. Duck Piralen
41. Backwater Duck Piralen

1. Kerala Meat Fry with Coconut Bits

This spiced, fried meat (usually beef), or erachiullarthu, is a staple in most Syrian-Christian homes and a 'special' on the menus of toddy shops and five-star hotels alike. The sliced coconut pieces add a delicious crunch.

Serves: 8

INGREDIENTS

Meat: 1 kg

Shallots, sliced: ½ cup

Ginger, sliced: 2 tsp

Garlic, sliced: 8 cloves

Coriander powder: 1 tbsp

Chilli powder: ¾ tbsp

Turmeric powder: ½ tsp

Aniseed: 1 tsp

Peppercorns: 1 tsp

Star anise: 2

Cinnamon: 2-inch piece

Cloves: 3

Cardamom: 2

Curry leaves: 1 sprig

Vinegar: 1 tbsp

Hot water: 1 cup

Salt: 1½ tsp

Coconut, sliced into 1-inch pcs: ½ cup

Turmeric: A pinch

Oil: ½ cup

Chopped onions: 2

METHOD

1. Wash, clean and cut the meat into 1-inch pieces.

2. Grind chilli, coriander and turmeric powders with aniseed, peppercorns, star anise, cinnamon, cloves and cardamom and make a paste. Set aside.

3. Coat the finely sliced coconut pieces with turmeric powder and salt, and shallow fry. Set aside.

4. Place meat in a pressure cooker and add the ground ingredients along with shallots, garlic, ginger and curry leaves. Lastly, add hot water, vinegar and salt. Mix well and leave to cook on low flame for 3 whistles. Turn off the flame and wait until the steam escapes. Open the lid and cook until the meat is coated with thick gravy.

5. Heat a wok with oil and add chopped onions. Fry until light brown. Add the cooked meat and slow fry until dry. Finally, add the fried coconut pieces and mix well. Serve hot.

2. Meat Stew

Stew made with chicken, mutton or beef, usually served with appam, is definitely a signature dish, during festivals or on special occasions in Kerala. The subtle blend of whole spices, curry leaves, chillies and creamy coconut milk makes this dish a very popular one.

Serves: 10

INGREDIENTS

Mutton or chicken: 1 kg

Potatoes: 3

Cinnamon: 2-inch piece

Cloves: 6

Cardamoms: 4

Peppercorns: 1 tbsp

Onions, sliced: 1 cup

Garlic, sliced: 1 tbsp

Ginger, sliced: 1 tbsp

Green chillies, slit: 6

Curry leaves: 1 stem

Vinegar: 1 tbsp

Coconut, grated to extract milk: 3½ cups

   First extract: ¾ cup

   Second extract: 3 cups

Oil: ¼ cup

Salt to taste

To season

Shallots, finely sliced: 2

Dry red chilli, cut into half: 1

Mustard seeds: ½ tsp

Curry leaves: 1 sprig

Tomato, sliced: 1

METHOD

1. Wash and clean the meat and trim the fat. Cut into medium-sized pieces. Peel the potatoes and cut them into wedges.

2. In a heavy-bottomed wok, heat oil and add cinnamon, cloves, cardamom, peppercorns and curry leaves. Add the onions, ginger, garlic and green chillies. Sauté till the onions turn soft and golden.

3. Add the meat and fry gently until light brown, add vinegar, the second extract of coconut milk and salt. Leave to simmer on a low flame.

4. When the meat is half cooked, add the potato wedges, cover the wok and let it cook. Once the meat is tender and the gravy has reduced, add the first extract of coconut milk. Bring to a boil and remove from flame.

5. Heat 2 tsp oil in a wok and splutter mustard seeds. Add shallots, dry red chilli, curry leaves and stir until light brown. Pour this into the stew.

6. Before serving, garnish with sliced tomatoes.

Note: Do not let the stew boil for long after adding the first extract of coconut milk as it could curdle. Serve hot.

3. Meat Pattichu Varathathu

Meat cooked dry with spices is an all-time favourite, also served as a starter.

Serves: 8

INGREDIENTS

Meat: 1 kg

Coriander powder: 1 tbsp

Chilli powder: ½ tbsp

Turmeric powder: ¼ tsp

Pepper powder: ½ tsp

Garlic, sliced: 1 tsp and extra 6 cloves

Aniseed: ½ tsp

Cinnamon: 1-inch piece

Cloves: 2

Vinegar: 1 tbsp

Salt to taste

Ginger, chopped: 1½ tsp

Hot water: 2 cups

Potatoes, cubed: 2

For tempering

Oil: 2 tbsp

Mustard seeds: ¼ tsp

Shallots, sliced: 2 tbsp

METHOD

1. Wash and clean the meat, and cut into large cubes.

2. Grind chilli, coriander, turmeric and pepper powders, aniseed, garlic, cloves and cinnamon to a fine paste.

3. Marinate the meat with the ground paste. To this, add chopped ginger, vinegar and salt and keep aside for 1 hour.

4. Cook the marinated meat in 2 cups hot water. When the meat is half cooked, add the potatoes and garlic.

5. When the potatoes are done and the gravy is thick, remove from the flame.

6. Heat a wok with oil and splutter mustard seeds. Add shallots and stir until light brown.

7. Add the cooked meat and potatoes and stir gently. Make sure the potatoes do not break. When the gravy doesn't stick to the sides of the pan, remove from flame and serve hot.

4. Mutton Chops

Succulent meat on the bone, coated with a thick gravy, can be served for any occasion.

Serves: 8

INGREDIENTS

Mutton with bone: 1 kg

Onion, finely chopped: ¾ cup

Garlic paste: ½ tsp

Ginger paste: ½ tsp

Chilli powder: ¾ tsp

Pepper powder: ½ tsp

Turmeric powder: ¼ tsp

Cumin powder: ½ tsp

Cloves, powdered: 2

Cinnamon, powdered: 2-inch piece

Cardamom, powdered: 2

Lime juice: 1 tbsp

Water: ½ cup

Oil: ¼ cup

Salt: 1 tsp

METHOD

1. Wash the mutton and cut it into 2-inch pieces, taking care to keep the meat on the bone.

2. Transfer the mutton to a pan, add ½ cup water and salt and cook on a low flame. When done, drain the stock and reserve it.

3. Heat oil in a pan and add the chopped onion. Fry until golden brown. Add the ginger and garlic pastes. Stir until light brown.

4. Make a paste of chilli, pepper and turmeric powders, and add to the browned ingredients.

5. Fry on a low flame until the oil separates. Add the mutton pieces, stir until brown. Pour in the reserved meat stock and lime juice and leave to simmer for 10 minutes.

6. Add the powdered cumin, cloves, cinnamon and cardamom. Mix well. Once the gravy has thickened, remove from flame. Serve hot.

5. Mutton Piralen

The combination of spices elevates this dish from ordinary to special.

Serves: 8

INGREDIENTS

Mutton: 1 kg

Onions, sliced: 2, big

Coconut, grated (to extract milk): 3 cups

    1st extract: ½ cup

    2nd extract: 2 cups

Salt to taste

Grind together

Red chillies, deseeded: 12

Ginger: 1-inch piece

Garlic: 1 pod

Peppercorns: ½ tsp

Coriander powder: 1 tsp

Khus Khus (poppy seeds), soaked in water: 1 tsp

Cinnamon: 2

Cloves: 6

Aniseed: 1 tsp

Shallots: 3 tsp

Mustard seeds: ¼ tsp

METHOD

1. Wash, clean and cut the mutton into medium-sized pieces.

2. Grind the ingredients mentioned into a fine paste and set aside.

3. Heat oil in a wok and fry the onions to a brown colour. Remove the onions from oil and set aside. Into the same oil add the ground paste and sauté on a low flame. When the oil separates, add the meat pieces and salt and sauté again. Mix half the quantity of the browned onions. Pour the 2nd extract of coconut milk. Stir well and cook on medium flame until the meat is cooked. Add the 1st extract of coconut milk and bring to a boil. Mix well. Garnish with the remaining browned onions. Serve hot.

6. Mutton Chilli Fry

Chunks of juicy, tender mutton soaked in spicy goodness could tickle any palate.

Serves: 8

INGREDIENTS

Mutton: 1 kg

Cloves: 8

Cardamom: 3

Cinnamon: 1-inch piece

Oil: ¼ cup

Onion, finely chopped: 1

Garlic, finely sliced: 12 cloves

Dry red chillies, broken into
4 pcs: 8

Pepper powder: 1 tbsp

Turmeric powder: A pinch

Tomato, chopped: ½ cup

Warm water: 1 cup

Salt to taste

METHOD

1. Wash, clean and cut the mutton into 1-inch pieces. Roast and powder the cloves, cardamom and cinnamon.

2. Heat oil in a pan and sauté the powdered ingredients. Add onion, garlic, red chillies, pepper and turmeric powders one by one and sauté well. Finally, add tomatoes and mix well.

3. When the tomatoes are done, add the mutton pieces and sauté again. Add salt and warm water, and cook the meat.

4. When the meat is done and the gravy coats the mutton, remove from flame. Serve hot.

7. Mutton Bafath

This was one of my mother's early recipes that made its debut in the newly launched cookery columns of Malayala Manorama and has remained a family favourite.

Serves: 10

My mother told me that the best years of her early life were spent in Mumbai, which gave her the opportunity to hone her talents. She also learnt Bharatanatyam and Rabindra Sangeet under a Bengali master. It was in Mumbai that she came to be recognized for her recipes, much to everyone's delight.

INGREDIENTS

Mutton: ½ kg

Warm water: 1½ cups

Salt to taste

Dry red chillies, deseeded: 6

Ginger: ½ inch piece

Garlic cloves: 6

Cardamom: 3

Cloves: 3

Cinnamon: 1-inch piece

Vinegar: ¼ cup

Salt: ½ tsp

Carrots, sliced: ¾ cup

Green peas: ¾ cup

Potatoes: medium-sized, peeled and cut into fingers

Shallots, sliced: 1 tbsp

Oil: ½ cup

Tomatoes: ¾ cup

Coconut milk, from half a coconut: 2 cups

Curry leaves: 2 sprigs

METHOD

1. Wash, clean and cut the mutton into medium-sized pieces. Add salt and pressure-cook the mutton with 1½ cups warm water for 4 whistles. After the mutton is cooked, there should be ½ cup of stock left in the pan.

2. Grind red chillies, ginger, garlic, cardamom, cloves and cinnamon with vinegar to a paste. Set aside.

3. Cook carrots first in 1 cup water and ¼ tsp salt. When the carrots are half done, add green peas. Remove from the flame before they are fully cooked.

4. Parboil potatoes with ¼ tsp salt and set aside.

5. Heat oil in a pan and sauté the cooked mutton and set aside. In the same pan, fry the potatoes. Set aside. Add the sliced shallots and fry till brown. Add the ground paste and sauté until the oil separates. Add the cooked vegetables and fried potatoes. Stir for a minute. Add the cooked mutton, and fry for 3 more minutes. Add the stock and the tomato wedges and let it simmer until the tomatoes are lightly cooked. Finally, add the coconut milk and curry leaves.

6. Once the steam starts to appear, remove from flame.

8. Mutton Red Curry

A spicy and flavourful gravy-based dish that appeals to young and old, and goes well with both rice and chapatis.

Serves: 10

INGREDIENTS

Mutton: 1 kg

Ginger: 2-inch piece

Garlic: 1 pod

Chilli powder: 2 tbsp

Cumin seeds: ½ tbsp

Fenugreek seeds: ½ tsp

Turmeric powder: ¼ tsp

Mustard seeds: ½ tsp

Oil: ¾ cup

Onions, sliced: 4 big

Tomatoes, big, skinned and chopped: 3

Vinegar: 2 tsp

Salt to taste

Sugar: 1 tsp

Tender coconut, finely sliced pcs for garnishing (optional)

Warm water: ¼ cup

METHOD

1. Wash, clean and cut the mutton with bone into medium pieces. Grind ginger, garlic, chilli and turmeric powders, cumin, fenugreek and mustard seeds to a fine paste.

2. Heat oil in a pan. Fry onions until brown and remove from flame. In the same pan, add the ground paste and sauté well till the oil separates. Add tomatoes and continue sautéing. Add the meat and sauté well till the water is absorbed. Add vinegar, salt, warm water and the fried onions. Mix well, cover the pan, and cook on a low flame.

3. Transfer all these items to a pressure cooker. Cook for 3 whistles. Once the meat is tender and the gravy is thick, add sugar. Mix well. Scatter pieces of tender coconut on top.

9. Mutton Kurma

Yoghurt, ground coconut and nuts add to the richness of the kurma and make it different from other curries with the same spices. Best paired with ghee rice or parottas.

Serves: 10

INGREDIENTS

Mutton: 1 kg

Cinnamon: 2-inch piece

Cloves: 7

Cardamom pods: 7

Star anise: 3

Onion, big, roughly chopped: 1

Turmeric powder: ½ tsp

Coriander leaves, chopped: A bunch

Hot water: 1 cup

Salt: 1½ tsp

Oil: ½ cup

Onions, sliced: 3

Ghee: 2 heaped tbsp

Ginger, sliced: 2 tbsp

Garlic cloves: 2 tbsp

Coriander powder: 1½ tbsp

Chilli powder: 1 tbsp

Turmeric powder: ½ tsp

METHOD

1. Wash and clean the mutton. Trim the excess fat, and cut into 2-inch cubes.

2. Put the mutton in a pressure cooker with the cinnamon, cloves, cardamoms, star anise, chopped onion, turmeric powder and salt. Pour 1½ cups hot water and cook on a low flame for 4 whistles.

3. When the mutton is tender and there are 2 cups of stock, take it off the flame and set aside.

4. Mix coriander, chilli and turmeric powders with a little water to form a paste. Set aside.

5. Grind the cashew nuts and grated coconut to a fine paste.

6. Heat oil in a wok and add sliced onions. Fry until brown, drain the oil and set aside.

7. Heat ghee in another pan and fry the ginger and garlic. When brown, add the coriander and chilli paste, and sauté well.

8. Add the chopped tomatoes and sauté till oil rises to the surface.

Tomatoes, chopped: 4

Green chillies, slit: 4

Beaten curd: ½ cup

Mint leaves, chopped: ¾ cup

Coriander leaves, chopped:
¾ cup

Coconut, ground into a paste:
½ cup

Cashew nuts, ground into a
paste: ¼ cup

Lime juice: 1 tbsp

9. Mix the beaten curd, coriander leaves, mint leaves and slit green chillies. Stir well. Add three-quarters of the fried onions and cooked mutton with its stock, stir and leave to simmer on a low flame till the meat and gravy are well blended. Add the cashew nut and coconut pastes to the curry, and mix well. At this stage, add lime juice, salt to taste and remove from flame. Garnish with the rest of the fried onions and serve hot.

10. Meatball Curry

This simple dish can be relished with just about anything from puttu to chapatis.

Serves: 8

INGREDIENTS

For the meatballs
Meat, minced: ½ kg

Chilli powder: 1 tsp

Coriander powder: 3 tsp

Turmeric powder: ½ tsp

Pepper powder: ½ tsp

Aniseed: 1 tsp

Shallots, finely chopped: 2 tbsp

Green chillies, finely chopped: ½ tbsp

Ginger, finely chopped: ½ tbsp

Garlic, finely chopped: ½ tbsp

Salt: 1 tsp

For the gravy
Oil: ¼ cup

Onions, sliced: 1¼ cups

Ginger, sliced: 1 tsp

Garlic, sliced: 1¼ tsp

Green chillies, slit: 2

METHOD

1. Wash and clean the minced meat. Leave in a colander to drain. Ensure the meat is completely free of water.

2. Grind the chilli, coriander, turmeric and pepper powders along with aniseed, cinnamon and cardamom to a fine paste.

3. Take 2 tsp of this ground paste and mix with the minced meat. Keep the remaining paste to make the gravy.

4. To the minced meat, add shallots, green chillies, ginger, garlic and salt, and mix well. Make 1-inch-sized round meatballs and set aside.

For the gravy

1. In a heavy-bottomed pan, heat oil. Add the sliced onions, ginger, garlic and green chillies. Sauté well. Add the ground paste which was kept aside. Fry this well till the oil separates. Add curry leaves, vinegar and salt. Add the 2nd extract of coconut milk. When the gravy boils and starts to bubble, gently drop the meatballs one by one into the gravy, ensuring that they do not break.

Curry leaves: 1 sprig

Vinegar: ¾ tbsp

Grated coconut (to extract milk): 3 cups

1st extract of coconut milk: ¾ cup

2nd extract of coconut milk: 2 cups

Salt to taste

2. Continue cooking on a low flame without a lid till the meatballs have cooked through. The gravy should be reduced by half at this stage.

3. Now add the 1st extract of coconut milk and bring the curry to a quick boil. Remove from the flame and serve hot.

11. Roasted Raan

Raan generally means the leg of lamb, but in India, goat meat is preferred. Raan is a rustic dish with nomadic origins and has to be slow-cooked for best results.

Serves: 6

INGREDIENTS

Lean leg of lamb: 1 kg

Ginger paste: 1 tbsp

Garlic paste: 1 tbsp

Cumin seeds: 2 tsp

Aniseed: 2 tsp

Chilli powder: 2 tsp

Cinnamon: 2-inch piece

Salt to taste

Juice from two limes

Ghee: 3 tbsp

METHOD

1. Preheat the oven to 150°F.

2. Wash, clean and dry the leg of lamb. Poke holes in the meat with a fork. Grind cumin seeds, aniseed, chilli powder and cinnamon into a paste. Mix ginger and garlic pastes, salt and lime juice. Coat this paste all over the leg of the lamb and marinate for 5 hours.

3. Wrap the lamb in aluminium foil and bake in an oven preheated to 150°F for 2 hours. In between, unwrap the foil and baste the meat with butter turning the piece over twice or thrice. After 2 hours, use a tester or sharp skewer to see if the meat is cooked. Once done, reduce the temperature to 100°F. Scrape the sediments, mix with ghee and coat the lamb's leg with the paste. Place back in the oven for another 10 minutes till it is light brown.

4. While serving, place the raan in a flat dish with onion rings, sliced cucumber and sliced tomatoes.

Note: Serve with mint and raisin chutney (recipe on page 70).

12. Veal Roast

This is a succulent, tender roast with a delicious gravy. Creamy mashed potatoes go perfectly with it though it can also be served with a side of buttered carrots and sweet green peas.

Serves: 8

INGREDIENTS

Veal (tender beef): 1 kg, single piece

Pepper powder: 2 tsp

Garlic, crushed: 1 tsp

Honey: 1 tbsp

Olive oil: 2 tbsp

Butter: 1 tsp

Cornflour: 1 tbsp

Coriander leaves, crushed: 2 tbsp

Salt to taste

Meat stock: 2 cups

(recipe on the next page)

METHOD

1. Wash and clean the meat, pat it dry and place in a shallow dish. Poke it with a fork all over. Make a marinade by mixing pepper powder, garlic, honey, olive oil and salt. Marinate the meat and keep it overnight in the refrigerator.

2. The next morning, tie the meat with a string and place it in a pressure cooker. Add the stock and the remaining marinade, and cook for 4 whistles. Reduce the flame and simmer for 45 minutes till the meat is done. Remove from the flame.

3. Take a wide and thick-bottomed pan, and place the cooked meat in it. Carefully brown the meat all over and set aside.

4. In the same pan, melt 1 tsp of butter and add 1 tbsp cornflour. Sauté well and add the gravy along with the brown bits left in the cooker. Stir well to make a sauce.

For the mashed potatoes

Potatoes, boiled and mashed:
2 heaped cups

Butter: 50 g

Milk: 1 cup

Salt to taste

For the meat stock

Mutton or chicken bones: 1 kg

Onions, chopped: 4

Water: 24 cups

Salt to taste

5. To prepare mashed potatoes, beat butter and blend well into the potatoes. Add the milk little by little to get the right creamy consistency. Add salt to taste.

6. Place the cooked meat on a flat board and slice it thinly and evenly. To plate, take a flat dish and place the mashed potatoes in the middle. Arrange the meat slices around the mashed potatoes. Before serving, drizzle some sauce on the meat pieces.

METHOD
For the meat stock

1. Place the meat bones and onions in a large pressure cooker. Add about 24 cups of water and salt to taste. Cook on medium flame for 3 whistles. Lower the flame and allow it to simmer for 10 minutes. Remove from the flame and wait for the pressure to be released from the cooker. Pass the stock through a cheesecloth placed on a fine sieve and freeze. This is a simple stock.

Note: Do not use too many seasonings as it will affect the taste of the final dish.

13. Veal Chops

Veal is much sought after for its flavour. The spices and other ingredients only enhance its taste.

Yields: 12

INGREDIENTS

Meat with bone (chops): 1 kg

Ginger: 1-inch piece

Garlic pod: 1

Chilli powder: 1 tbsp

Cumin seeds: 1 tbsp

Worcestershire sauce: 2 tbsp

Soy sauce: 2 tbsp

Juice of 1 big lemon

Onions, thinly sliced: 3

Baby potatoes: 10

Baby carrots: 8

Salt to taste

Oil: ½ cup

METHOD

1. Wash and clean the meat chops and pat them dry.

2. Grind ginger, garlic, chilli powder and cumin seeds. Add Worcestershire sauce, soy sauce, juice of one lime and salt. Coat this marinade on the chops along with half the thinly sliced onions. Keep this for 6 hours.

3. Heat oil in a wok. Fry the remaining sliced onions to a light brown colour and set aside. In the same oil, add the chops and fry until brown. Transfer the chops to a pressure cooker. Add the leftover marinade and fried onions with 2 cups warm water. Blend all the ingredients and cook till the meat is tender.

4. Transfer the meat chops to a wok and sauté once more. Remove from the flame. Serve with baby potatoes and diced carrots sautéed in butter.

14. Roast Beef

This is gourmet fare, yet another family favourite.

Serves: 12

INGREDIENTS

Beef: 1 kg, single piece

Garlic, sliced: 1 tbsp

Ginger, sliced: 1 tsp

Mustard seeds: ¼ tsp

Peppercorns: ½ tsp

Salt: 1 tsp

Vinegar: 2 tsp

Cloves: 8

Onions, sliced: ¼ cup

Oil: 3 tbsp

Ghee: 1 tbsp

Flour: 1½ tsp

Boiling hot water: 5–6 cups

METHOD

1. Wash, clean and leave the beef to drain and dry. Prick the meat all over with a fork.

2. Grind garlic, ginger, mustard seeds and peppercorns with vinegar. Add salt and marinate the beef. Insert the whole cloves into the beef randomly. Marinate for 5 hours.

3. Soak the sliced onion in salt water and squeeze dry. Set aside.

4. In a large wok, heat oil and ghee together. Add the onion and sauté until golden brown.

5. Dust the marinated beef with 1 tsp flour. Reserve the remaining flour. Add the beef to the sautéed onions and turn at regular intervals until lightly fried. When the meat has browned evenly, sprinkle the remaining flour over the meat. Once the flour has browned, pour boiling hot water into the pan. The beef should be completely submerged in the water. Cover with a lid and leave to cook on a low flame.

6. When the meat is tender and the gravy thick, remove from the flame. Lift the meat from the pan and place it on a wooden board. Slice the meat. Arrange the meat on a flat serving dish and pour the gravy over it. Serve hot.

15. Beef Chops

A favourite that has stood the test of time, both in our family and with guests.

Yields: 10

INGREDIENTS

Beef: 1 kg

Coriander powder: 2 tsp

Chilli powder: 1 tsp

Cumin powder: ½ tsp

Turmeric powder: ¼ tsp

Peppercorns, crushed: ½ tsp

Aniseed, crushed: A pinch

Ginger, sliced: 1 tsp

Garlic, sliced: 2 tsp

Onions, sliced: 1 cup

Cloves, powdered: ½ tsp

Cinnamon, powdered: ½ tsp

Lime juice: 1 tbsp

Salt: 1½ tsp

Oil: ½ cup

Onions, chopped: 1 cup

Hot water: 2 cups

For garnishing

Mint leaves: 1 tsp

Coriander leaves: 1 tsp

Lemon wedges: 6

METHOD

1. Wash and clean the beef. Then, slice it in ½ inch thick 3-inch squares.

2. Using a meat mallet, gently pound the beef slices. When one side is done, flip it over and repeat. Be careful not to tear or mash up the meat.

3. In a large bowl, mix the coriander, chilli, cumin and turmeric powders along with crushed pepper, aniseed, ginger, garlic, powdered cloves, cinnamon, lime juice and salt. Spread the marinade on the pounded beef squares and leave to marinate for 2 hours.

4. Heat half the oil in a wok and fry onions until golden brown. Remove from oil and set aside. Add the remaining oil and fry the marinated beef in batches, taking care not to crowd the pan. Remove from oil and set aside.

5. After all the slices are fried, pour the leftover marinade into a pan. Add 2 cups of hot water and leave it to boil.

6. Once it starts boiling, slip in the fried beef slices and fried onions. Cover the pan with a lid and leave it to cook on a low flame.

7. Once the meat is cooked and the meat slices are coated with gravy, remove from the flame. Serve in a flat dish and garnish with chopped mint or coriander leaves. Place a ring of lime wedges around the beef chops.

Note: Pounding a steak with a mallet is a great way to tenderize. There are two sides of a typical meat mallet; one side has teeth, the other is flat. For tenderizing, use the toothy side. It breaks through the fibres and softens the meat.

16. Beef Steak

This recipe is quite different from its counterpart in the West and has been customized for local tastes.

Serves: 6

INGREDIENTS

Beef slices: ½ kg

Pepper: 2 tsp

Mustard paste: ½ tsp

Garlic, crushed: 1 tsp

Onions: 2, medium-sized

Oil: ¼ cup

Butter: 1 tsp

Refined flour: 2 levelled tbsp

Worcestershire sauce: 2 tbsp

Ginger, sliced: 1-inch piece

Warm water: 3 cups

Salt to taste

METHOD

1. Wash and clean the beef slices, drain the water and keep aside.

2. Marinate the beef slices with salt, pepper, mustard paste and crushed garlic. Slice the onions thinly. Heat oil in a pan and fry the onions to a golden colour and set aside. Make a paste with flour and butter, and coat the meat with it.

3. Heat a pan with 2 tbsp oil. Add the meat and keep stirring for some time. Add 2 tbsp of Worcestershire sauce, ginger, half of the fried onions and the leftover marinade of the meat. Stir in 3 cups of warm water and cook the meat. Cook till the gravy becomes thick and covers the meat. Serve hot.

4. While serving, garnish the meat with the leftover fried onions.

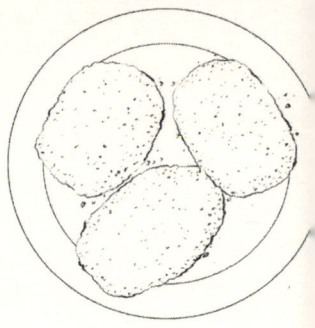

17. Masala Cutlet

Cutlets were a hot favourite in our home. They formed part of picnic baskets and
dinner parcels when we travelled overnight by train.

Yields: 12

INGREDIENTS

Meat, minced: ½ kg

Oil: 2 tbsp

Onions, chopped: 1 cup

Green chillies, chopped: 2 tbsp

Ginger, chopped: 1 tbsp

Vinegar: 1 tbsp

Salt to taste

Pepper powder: 1 tsp

Cloves, powdered: ½ tsp

Cinnamon, powdered: ½ tsp

Cardamom, powdered: ¼ tsp

Mashed potato: 1 cup

Eggs: 2

Breadcrumbs: ¼ cup

Oil: ½ cup

METHOD

1. Wash the minced meat and leave it to drain.

2. In a heavy-bottomed pan, heat 2 tbsp oil. Sauté onions, green chillies and
    ginger. When the onions start to turn brown, add the minced meat, vinegar
    and salt.

3. Cover the pan and leave the meat to cook. Do not add water as there will be
    enough in the meat. Stir at intervals to prevent lumps from forming. After the
    meat is cooked, add pepper, cloves, cinnamon and cardamom powders. Mix
    well and remove from the flame.

4. Once the minced meat has cooled sufficiently, mix in the mashed potato. Add
    the yolks from the eggs and reserve the whites.

5. Mix all the ingredients together, checking if the salt is adequate. Make small-
    sized balls of the minced meat mixture and flatten them a little.

6. Whisk the egg whites till light and frothy. Keep aside. In a separate dish,
    spread the breadcrumbs.

7. Dip the flattened cutlets in the egg white and then roll in the breadcrumbs till
    evenly coated. Once all the cutlets have been coated with breadcrumbs, they
    are ready for frying.

8. In a heavy-bottomed wok, heat oil and deep fry the cutlets in small batches.
    Serve hot.

18. Kola Balls with Mint and Raisin Chutney

My mother spent her childhood mostly in Tamil Nadu and Andhra Pradesh and that meant myriad regional culinary influences. Kola balls, or kola urundai, originated in Tamil Nadu. Aniseed adds an aromatic flavour to the urundai that are crispy outside and juicy inside. They make a delicious side dish or can be served as a snack.

Yields: 20

INGREDIENTS

Mutton, minced: ½ kg

Veal, minced: ½ kg

Roasted Bengal gram, powdered coarsely: 1 cup

Coconut, finely shredded: 1 cup

Coriander leaves, chopped: A handful

Mint leaves, chopped: A handful

Onions, minced: 2

Ginger, finely minced: 1 tbsp

Garlic cloves, minced: 3

Green chillies, minced: 4

Cinnamon: 1-inch piece

Clove: 1

Cardamom pods: 3

Aniseed: 1 tsp

Chilli powder: 1 tsp

Pepper, coarsely powdered: 1 tbsp

Bread without the crust, soaked in water and squeezed: 2 slices

Oil: 2 cups

Salt to taste

METHOD

1. Dry roast and powder cinnamon, clove, cardamom and aniseed. Mix all the other ingredients with the minced meat and roll into small balls. Fry in hot oil and serve with mint and raisin chutney.

Mint and Raisin Chutney

INGREDIENTS

Mint leaves: 1½ cups

Raisins: ½ cup

Chilli powder: 1 tbsp

Lime juice according to taste

Salt to taste

METHOD

1. Grind all the ingredients into a smooth paste and serve with the kola balls.

19. Mutton Liver Fry

The secret to a perfect liver fry is the cooking time. Make sure not to overcook.

Serves: 6

INGREDIENTS

Mutton liver: ½ kg

Turmeric powder: 1 tsp

Water: 1½ cups

Salt to taste

Onions, sliced: 2

Green chillies, slit: 5

Ginger, sliced: 1-inch piece

Chilli powder: ½ tbsp

Coriander powder: 1 tbsp

Pepper powder, freshly ground: 2 tsp

Turmeric powder: ½ tsp

Spice powder: 1 tsp

Thick coconut milk, extracted from the gratings of half a coconut: 1 cup

Oil: ½ cup

For the spice powder

Cinnamon stick: 1

Cloves: 5

Cardamom pods: 5

Aniseed: 1 tsp

METHOD

1. Wash the liver and place in a pressure cooker. Add water, turmeric powder and salt to taste. Cook till the liver is soft. Drain the water. Once cold, slice the liver into one-inch-long thin pieces. Set aside.

2. Heat oil in a wok. Sauté onions, green chillies and ginger.

3. Make a paste of chilli, coriander, pepper, turmeric powders and spice powder with a little water.

4. Add this paste to the sautéed ingredients. Fry on medium flame till the oil appears on the top. Add the sliced liver and mix well. Pour coconut milk and add salt to taste. Cook till the coconut milk is absorbed. Sauté till the liver pieces are semi-dry. Serve hot.

METHOD
For the spice powder

1. Gently roast all the ingredients and powder in a grinder. It can be stored for a few weeks in an airtight container.

20. Pork Vindaloo

The vindaloo made its way to India along with Portuguese explorers. More popular among the Christian community in Goa, it has become a favourite in Kerala too, especially in the central region.

Serves: 6

INGREDIENTS

Pork: ½ kg

Ginger paste: 2 tbsp

Garlic paste: 2 tbsp

Kashmiri chilli powder: 2 tbsp

Cumin seeds: 2 tsp

Mustard seeds: ½ tsp

Turmeric powder: ½ tsp

Fenugreek seeds: ¼ tsp

Peppercorns: 5-6

Tomatoes. blanched and minced: 2, big

Salt: 1½ tsp

Vinegar: 1 tbsp

Oil: ½ cup

Onions, sliced: 1 cup

Ginger, sliced: 2 tsp

Garlic cloves: 10

Sugar: 1 tsp

Vinegar: 1 tsp

METHOD

1. Wash, clean and cut the pork into 2-inch cubes. Retain some fat.

2. Grind chilli powder, cumin seeds, fenugreek seeds, mustard seeds, turmeric powder and peppercorns and set aside.

3. In a heavy-bottomed pan, heat oil and add sliced onions. Fry until brown and set aside. In the same pan, sauté the ginger and garlic pastes until the oil starts separating. Add the ground paste and sauté again. Add tomatoes. Once the oil starts to separate, add the pork pieces, half the vinegar and salt. Add ½ cup of hot water, cover with a lid to contain water and cook on a low flame. Once the meat is nearly cooked, add the sliced ginger, garlic cloves and fried onions. When the meat is tender, add 1 tsp sugar mixed with the remaining vinegar. Mix well and remove from the flame. Serve.

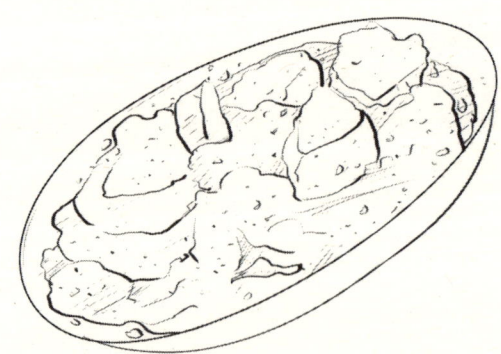

Kappa Bonda

Parippuvada

Vatteyappam

Assorted Fritters

Groundnut Chikki, Kuzhalappam,
Murukku, Avalos Unda, Pakkavada,
Achappam

Date Sweet

Assorted Kerala Sweets

Coffee Cake

Rich Fruit Cake

Palappam with Vegetable Stew

Vellayappam

Idiyappam

Puttu

Ney Pathiri

Uppumav

Parotta

Egg Roast

Egg Curry

Kerala Meat Fry

Mutton Bafath

Mutton Red Curry

Mutton Kurma

Veal Roast

Beef Steak

Trivandrum Chicken

Easter Chicken Roast

Mixed Meat Grill

Kuttanad Duck Curry

Duck Fry

Fish Fry

Fish Molee

Red Fish Curry

Vembanad Karimeen

Goan Fish Curry

Alleppey Fish Curry with Mangoes

Sardines Vattichathu

Lobster Fry

Prawn Mappas

Prawns in Lemon Garlic Sauce

Prawn Batter Fry

Dry Prawn and Mango Curry

Chilli Fish

Crab Ularth

Anchovy (Natholi) Crispies

21. Chicken Curry Country Style

The special taste and aroma of coconut milk that defines this curry takes you back to your mother's kitchen.

Serves: 10

INGREDIENTS

Chicken, cut into medium-sized pcs: 1 kg

Coriander powder: 1 heaped tbsp

Chilli powder: 2 tsp

Turmeric powder: ¼ tsp

Cinnamon: 2-inch piece

Cloves: 6

Cardamom: 4

Aniseed: 1 tsp

Potatoes: 4

Oil: ¼ cup

Onions, finely sliced: ½ cup

Ginger, julienned: 2 tsp

Garlic cloves: 8

Green chillies, slit: 6

Vinegar: 1 tbsp

Salt to taste

Coconut, grated, to extract milk: 1

   1st extract of coconut milk: 1 cup

   2nd extract of coconut milk: 3 cups

METHOD

1. Wash, clean and cut the chicken into medium-sized pieces.

2. Grind coriander, chilli and turmeric powders, cinnamon, cloves, cardamom and aniseed into a paste.

3. Peel and quarter the potatoes.

4. Heat oil, add the sliced onion, ginger, garlic and green chillies and fry until they are golden brown.

5. Add the ground paste and sauté. Add the chicken, vinegar and salt. Stir for 5 minutes and add the 2nd extract of coconut milk. Cover the pan with a well-fitting lid and cook the chicken.

6. When the chicken is nearly done, add the potatoes. After it is well cooked, add the 1st extract of coconut milk, and remove from the flame.

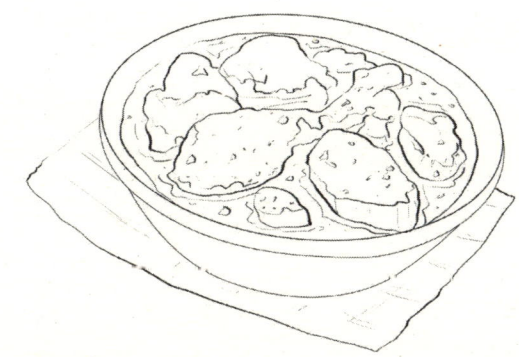

For tempering

Oil: 1 tbsp

Ghee: 1 tsp

Mustard seeds: 1 tsp

Shallots, sliced: 2 tbsp

Curry leaves: 2 sprigs

7. Heat oil and ghee in a pan. Splutter mustard seeds and lightly fry the shallots and curry leaves.

8. Add this tempering to the curry.

Note: The same recipe can be used to make duck and mutton curry too.

22. Trivandrum Chicken

When a new café called Trivandrum Corner opened in our home town, Kottayam, this was one of the special dishes there, which was promptly reproduced to crispy perfection in my mother's kitchen.

Serves: 8

INGREDIENTS

Chicken: 1 kg

Shallots: 10

Garlic cloves: 10

Ginger: 1-inch piece

Chilli powder: 2 tbsp

Aniseed: 1 tbsp

Rice flour: 4 tbsp

Lime juice: 2 tbsp

Coconut oil: ¼ kg

Salt: 1 tsp

METHOD

1. Wash, clean, cut the chicken into large pieces and make gashes on them.

2. Grind the shallots, ginger, garlic, aniseed and chilli powder together to make a smooth paste. Add lime juice and salt, and marinate the chicken in a cool place for 4 hours.

3. Heat oil in a wok. Sprinkle rice flour on the marinated chicken and fry in the hot oil. The residue of the fried flour should be drained and sprinkled on the chicken pieces. Serve hot.

Note: Coconut oil adds to the flavour, but may be replaced by any other oil.

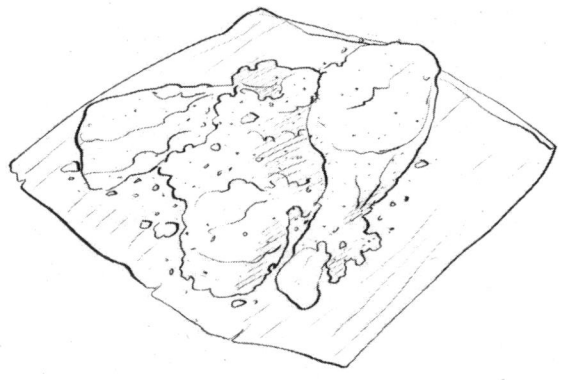

23. Masala Chicken

Roasted spices mark this curry out as something different.

Serves: 8

INGREDIENTS

Chicken: 1 kg

Pepper powder: 2 tsp

Vinegar: 2 tbsp

Salt to taste

Onions, chopped into small pcs: 4

Shallots, ground into a paste: 1 cup

Ginger paste: 100 g

Garlic paste: 1 pod

Coriander powder: 3 tsp

Chilli powder: 4 tsp

Fenugreek powder: ¾ tsp

Tomatoes, chopped into small pcs: 3

Powdered spices: 1 tsp

Oil: ¾ cup

Water: 2 cups

METHOD

1. Wash, clean and cut the chicken into large pieces. Make a paste of pepper powder, vinegar and salt. Marinate the chicken for half an hour.

2. Heat oil in a wok, lightly fry the pieces and set aside. In the same wok, fry onions until golden and remove. Add the ground shallots and sauté well. Add ginger paste followed by garlic paste. Sauté these well till the oil separates. Make a paste of coriander, chilli and fenugreek powders and add to the sautéed ingredients. Add chopped tomatoes and keep stirring on a low flame until the oil separates. Add water, and once it starts boiling, add the chicken pieces and fried onions. Cook until the meat is soft and the gravy is thick. Before removing from fire, sprinkle the spices powder. Mix well. Serve hot.

For the spices powder

1. Gently roast and grind to powder a 2-inch cinnamon piece, 4 cloves, 4 cardamoms and 1 tsp aniseed. This can be stored for later use too.

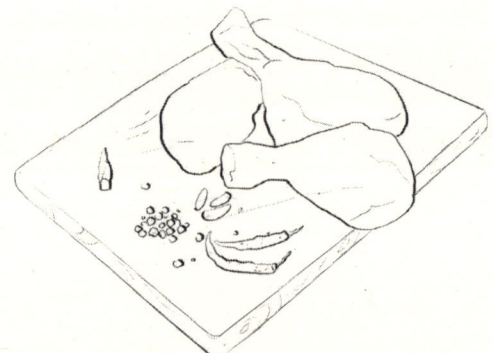

24. Ellu Chicken

The distinct and piquant flavour of sesame (ellu) elevates the rich flavour of this dish.

Serves: 6

INGREDIENTS

Chicken: 1 kg

Eggs: 2

Breadcrumbs: 1 cup

White and black sesame seeds: 3 tbsp

Garlic, chopped: 2 tsp

Ginger, chopped: 2 tsp

Green chillies: 6

Turmeric powder: 1 tsp

Peppercorns: 1 tsp

Lime juice: 2 tbsp

Hot water: 2 cups

Oil: ½ cup

Salt: 1 tsp

For the gravy

Butter: 1 tsp

Cornflour: 1 tsp

METHOD

1. Wash, clean and cut the chicken into 10 pieces. Mix the sesame seeds and breadcrumbs and set aside.

2. Grind garlic, ginger, green chillies, peppercorns and turmeric powder into a smooth paste. Add lime juice and marinate the chicken.

3. Place the chicken in a heavy-bottomed pan. Add hot water, salt and cook.

4. When the chicken is cooked, there should be ½ cup stock left for the gravy.

5. Separate the chicken pieces from the stock.

6. Beat the eggs. Dip the cooked chicken pieces in beaten eggs. Coat well by rolling in breadcrumbs mixed with sesame seeds.

7. Heat oil in a shallow pan and deep fry the chicken. Serve hot with a bowl of gravy.

8. To make the gravy, melt butter in a small pan. Add cornflour and when light brown, add the stock and stir to make a gravy.

Note: Mutton chops can also be used instead of chicken.

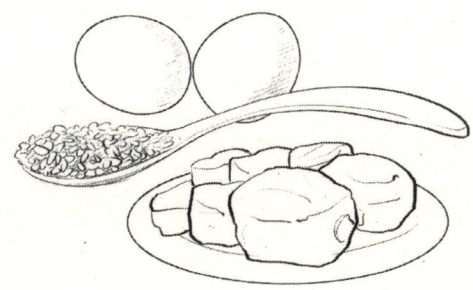

25. Pepper Chicken

There are variations of this recipe in different parts of south India and it remains a 'hot' favourite in homes and restaurants.

Serves: 8

INGREDIENTS

Chicken pcs: 1 kg

Peppercorns: ¾ tbsp

Garlic cloves: 1 heaped tbsp

Cumin seeds: ¾ levelled tbsp

Mustard seeds: ¾ tbsp

Onions, finely sliced: 2

Ginger, finely chopped:
1-inch piece

Green chillies, slit: 4

Salt to taste

METHOD

1. Wash, clean and cut the chicken into medium-sized pieces.

2. Grind together peppercorns, garlic cloves, cumin and mustard seeds.

3. Sauté onions, ginger and green chillies. Add the chicken pieces, salt and the ground paste, sauté until the oil separates. Add warm water and cook. Take care not to add too much water, so that when the chicken is cooked, the residual gravy is thick. Once cooked, the chicken pieces should be separated from the gravy.

4. Heat oil in a separate pan and sauté a couple of sliced onions, and lightly shallow fry the cooked chicken until brown. You could garnish the chicken with more fried onions and/or add a couple of cubed or thickly sliced and pan-fried potatoes.

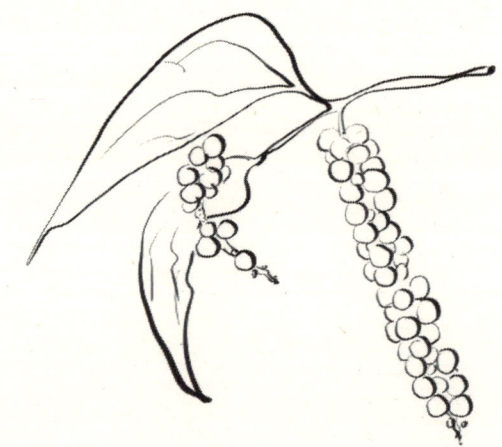

26. Chicken Piralen

Essentially a Kerala-style roast that uses a flavoursome blend of spices.

Serves: 8

INGREDIENTS

Chicken: 1 kg

Ginger: 1-inch piece

Garlic cloves: 8

Chilli powder: 1 tbsp

Turmeric powder: ½ tsp

Aniseed: 1 tsp

Cinnamon: 3-inch piece

Cloves: 3

Shallots: 10 + 1 cup

Salt to taste

Oil: ½ cup

METHOD

1. Wash, clean and cut the chicken into large pieces.

2. Grind chilli and turmeric powders, aniseed, cinnamon and cloves with 10 shallots. Add salt and coat the chicken pieces with the ground paste. Slice the rest of the shallots and add to the chicken. Cook on a low flame till the chicken is three-quarters done. Remove the pieces from the pan and reserve the gravy.

3. In a pan, heat oil. Add the chicken pieces and fry till they are golden brown. Now pour the reserved gravy over the fried chicken and mix until the gravy has coated the pieces well. Serve hot.

27. Murgh Masala

This is a north Indian recipe adapted for the Malayali palate.

Serves: 8

INGREDIENTS

Chicken: 1 kg

Chilli powder: 2 tsp

Coriander powder: ½ tsp

Salt to taste

Oil: ½ cup

Onions, chopped: 1 cup

Turmeric powder: 1 tsp

Ginger, ground: 2 tsp

Garlic, ground: ½ tsp

Peppercorns, crushed: 18

Tomatoes, finely chopped:
1½ cups

Tomato sauce: 1 tbsp

Curd: ¼ cup

Lime juice: 1 tsp

Coriander leaves: ¼ cup

METHOD

1. Wash, clean and cut the chicken into 10–12 pieces. Make a paste of the coriander, chilli and turmeric powders with a little water. Add salt to taste. Coat the chicken pieces with the paste and marinate for 1 hour.

2. Heat oil in a wok and brown the onions. When browned, add the ginger and garlic pastes, and sauté well. Add tomatoes, pepper and tomato sauce. Keep stirring till the oil clears on top. Mix in curd and lime juice and add the chicken pieces. Fry till the marinated pieces are browned on all sides. Add ½ cup warm water, place the lid and allow the chicken to cook. Garnish with chopped coriander and remove from the flame. Serve hot.

28. Murgh Mughlai

This recipe was put together after one of my mother's many visits to Delhi's iconic restaurants, Moti Mahal in Darya Ganj and Karim's in Nizamuddin.

Serves: 8

INGREDIENTS

Chicken: 1 kg

Saffron: A pinch

Milk: ¼ cup

Onions, sliced and squeezed in salt water: 2

Peppercorns: 10

Shallots: ¼ cup

Ginger: 1-inch piece

Garlic cloves: 6

Skin of dry red chillies: 4

Turmeric powder: ½ tsp

Tomatoes, chopped: 2

Juice of ½ a lime

Cinnamon: 1-inch piece

Cloves: 5

Cardamoms: 2

Hot water: ¼ cup

Salt to taste

Oil: ¼ cup

METHOD

1. Wash, clean and cut the chicken into medium-sized pieces.

2. Soak the strands of saffron in warm milk and keep it aside. Powder the cinnamon, cloves and cardamoms.

3. Grind shallots, ginger, garlic, red chillies and turmeric powder to make a paste.

4. Heat a pan with oil. Fry the peppercorns and add onions. Sauté well. Add the ground paste and sauté again. Add the chicken and keep stirring till the pieces are coated all over and lightly browned. Add the chopped tomatoes, lime juice, powdered spices and salt to taste, mix well. Add hot water, cover the pan with a lid and cook.

5. When the meat is tender, add the strained saffron milk. Allow to boil once and remove from the flame.

29. New Year Chicken Roast

My maternal grandfather, Dr George Philip, enjoyed good food. This New Year Roast was his creation. He was ably assisted by his cook 'Gunner' Unni, who had served in the British Indian Army during World War II. This dish was one of the many I enjoyed during my visits to my grandparents in Kollam.

Serves: 8

INGREDIENTS
Whole chicken: 1 kg

For the marinade
Chilli powder: ½ tsp

Coriander powder: 1 tsp

Cumin seeds: ½ tsp

Ginger: 1-inch piece

Garlic cloves: 8

Salt to taste

Grind the above ingredients and marinate the whole chicken for about 2 hours. Poke the chicken with a fork.

For the gravy
Onion, chopped: 1

Ginger, chopped: 1-inch piece

Green chillies, slit: 4

Pepper: 1 tsp

Garlic pod: 1

Turmeric powder: ¼ tsp

Chilli powder: 1½ tsp

Ghee: 2 tbsp

Cardamom pods: 4

METHOD
1. Heat oil in a wok. Fry bread cubes, cashew nuts and raisins, and keep them aside. In the same wok, sauté the onions, green chillies and ginger. Add the liver, potatoes, beaten egg and salt. Mix all the ingredients well. Add the fried bread cubes, cashew nuts and raisins. Stuff this filling into the cavity of the chicken. Stitch the rear end of the stomach cavity with a needle and twine.

2. Heat some more oil in the wok and brown the whole chicken by turning it around on all sides. Lift the chicken from the wok and keep it aside.

METHOD
1. Heat oil in a wok and lightly brown the onions.

2. Crush all the ingredients except the spices and shallots. Add the crushed ingredients to the browned onions and sauté well.

3. Heat ghee in a separate pan and lightly fry the shallots and spices. Add to the sautéed ingredients. Pour hot water, vinegar and add salt to taste. Once it starts to boil, add the fried chicken. Cover the wok and cook on medium flame.

4. When the meat becomes tender and the gravy thick, remove from the flame.

Cloves: 4

Cinnamon: 2-inch piece

Shallots, sliced: 10

Vinegar: 1 tbsp

Salt to taste

Hot water: 4 cups

For the stuffing

Oil: ½ cup

Bread, cut into cubes: 4 slices

Cashew nuts, chopped: 2 tbsp

Raisins: 1 tbsp

Onion, chopped: 1 big

Ginger, chopped: 1-inch piece

Green chillies, slit: 3

Coriander leaves: A bunch

Chicken liver, cooked,
chopped: 1 cup

Boiled and mashed potatoes:
1 cup

Egg, beaten: 1

Salt to taste

5. To serve this dish for a special occasion, present the whole roast on a large platter before carving.

6. Now remove the stitches and scoop out the stuffing.

7. Place the stuffing in the middle of the serving plate. Carve the chicken and place the pieces around the stuffing. Pour some gravy on the chicken and keep the remaining gravy in a small jug.

30. Chicken Roast with Sauces

Tender pieces of chicken, in a caramelized sugar and spices sauce, is yet another great dish.

Serves: 8

INGREDIENTS

Chicken, cut into large pcs:
1 kg

Tomato sauce: 2 tbsp

Worcestershire sauce: 2 tbsp

Soy sauce: 2 tsp

Chilli powder: ¾ tbsp

Pepper powder: 1 tsp

Juice of 1 lime

Salt to taste

Onions, cut into fairly thick
rings: 2

Potatoes, cut into 2-inch
cubes: 2

Oil: ½ cup

Hot water: 2 cups

Arrowroot powder: 1 tsp

Sugar: 2 tbsp

Warm water: ¼ cup

METHOD

1. Wash, clean and cut the chicken into large pieces and make gashes on it.

2. Make a paste of tomato sauce, soy sauce, Worcestershire sauce, chilli powder, pepper powder, lime juice and salt. Marinate the chicken with this paste and set aside for 3 hours.

3. Heat oil in a pan. Add onions and potatoes. Sauté the onions till they are transparent and lightly fry the potatoes. Drain and keep aside.

4. In the same oil, lightly fry the chicken pieces in batches, taking care not to crowd the pan. Remove the excess marinade. Mix the fried chicken pieces with the sautéed onions, potatoes and the remaining marinade. Add hot water and cook the chicken pieces. Once it is done well, remove with a slotted spoon and reserve the gravy.

5. Stir the arrowroot powder into the gravy. Once the gravy starts to thicken, add the chicken pieces. After the chicken is well coated with the gravy, remove from the flame.

6. Heat a pan and melt sugar to a caramel colour. Add warm water carefully and keep stirring to make a caramel syrup. Add a portion of the gravy and mix well. Pour the gravy on the chicken.

7. Serve the chicken on a platter along with onion rings and potatoes.

31. Easter Chicken Roast

A simple but delicious roast chicken that could make any day a feast day.

Serves: 8

INGREDIENTS

Whole chicken with the skin:
1 kg

Ginger: 1-inch piece

Garlic cloves: 8

Chilli powder: 1 tsp

Turmeric powder: ½ tsp

Cinnamon: 2-inch piece

Cloves: 6

Vinegar: 1 tbsp

Salt to taste

Oil: ¼ cup

Hot water: 1¼ cup

METHOD

1. Wash and pat dry the whole chicken thoroughly. Grind ginger, garlic, chilli powder, turmeric powder, cinnamon and cloves. Add vinegar and salt. Marinate the chicken and set aside for 3 hours.

2. Heat oil in a wok and brown the chicken over a low flame. Pour hot water over the chicken and cook on low flame until tender and the gravy thickens.

3. Serve on a platter with boiled vegetables on the side.

32. Chicken Roast with Pomegranate Seeds

Honey, pomegranate juice and rosemary lend a special flavour to this dish.

Serves: 8

INGREDIENTS

Whole chicken with skin: 1 kg

Pepper: 2 tbsp

Garlic cloves: 2 tbsp

Juice of 1 pomegranate

Rosemary: 1½ tbsp

Juice of 1 lime

Butter: 50 g

Honey: 1½ tbsp

Salt to taste

Oil: 1 tbsp

Shallots, sliced: 3

Pomegranate seeds: A few, for garnishing

Cornflour: 1 tsp

Garlic, chopped: 5-6

Water: ½ cup

Butter: 1 tsp

METHOD

1. Preheat the oven to 350°F.

2. Grind the pepper and garlic, and add pomegranate juice, rosemary, lime juice, butter and honey. Blend well. Add salt to taste.

3. Prick the chicken all over with a fork. Coat the whole chicken with the blended ingredients. Lift the skin and apply the marinade all over. Keep it aside for half an hour.

4. Place the chicken in a baking tray and cover with aluminium foil. Bake for 1 hour. Remove the foil and turn the chicken over. Take a pastry brush and baste the chicken with honey. Remove all the residue with the gravy from the chicken and use it to make the gravy.

5. Put the chicken in a separate pan and place it back in the oven for 15 minutes for the glaze to set and the skin to brown. This keeps the chicken moist inside and crispy outside.

For the gravy

1. Melt butter in a pan. Add chopped garlic and fry until light brown. Add ½ cup water and allow it to boil. Add the residue from the gravy and salt to taste. Stir well to make a thick gravy.

2. Place the chicken in a flat serving dish and carve it. Pour some gravy over the slices and garnish with pomegranate seeds.

33. Chicken with Puttu

Puttu can be eaten with a variety of savoury curries. This chicken curry is thickened with coconut milk.

Serves: 8

INGREDIENTS

Chicken: 1 kg

Chilli powder: 2 tsp

Coriander powder: 3 tbsp

Turmeric powder: 1 tsp

Aniseed: 1½ tsp

Peppercorns: 1 tsp

Cinnamon: 3 small pcs

Cloves: 6

Cardamom: 6

Star anise: 4

Onions, sliced: 4

Green chillies, slit: 2

Ginger, finely sliced: 1-inch piece

Salt to taste

Vinegar: 1 tbsp

Oil: 1 cup

Coconut, grated, to extract milk: 1

   1st extract by adding 1 cup water

   2nd extract of thin milk by adding 3 cups water

METHOD

1. Wash and clean the whole chicken and prick all over with a fork. Make a paste of ½ tsp chilli powder, ¼ tsp turmeric powder, salt and water and marinate the chicken for half an hour.

2. Grind the rest of the chilli powder, coriander powder, turmeric powder, pepper and aniseed along with cinnamon, cloves, cardamom and star anise. Set aside.

3. Heat oil in a wok. Fry the marinated chicken until all sides are brown. Remove and set aside. Add the remaining oil and sauté the onions, green chillies and ginger. Add the ground paste and fry on a low flame till the oil separates.

4. Pour the 2nd extract of coconut milk and mix well. Add vinegar and salt to taste. Put the chicken back into the pan and cook it on a low flame. Add salt to taste. Once the chicken is soft, pour the thick coconut milk. Mix well. Just as it begins to boil, remove from flame.

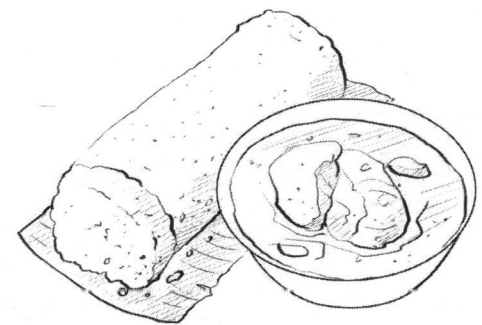

For tempering

Ghee: 2 tbsp

Mustard seeds: ½ tsp

Shallots, chopped: 4

Red chillies, cut into 6 pcs: 2

Curry leaves: 2 sprigs

To make the puttu

Coarse rice flour: 1 cup

Coconut, grated: ½ cup

Water as required

Salt to taste

To season

Oil: 2 tbsp

Mustard seeds: ½ tsp

Onion, chopped: 1

Green chillies, minced: 2

Ginger, minced: A small piece

Curry leaves, chopped: 1 sprig

METHOD

1. In a small wok, heat ghee and splutter mustard seeds. Add the chopped shallots, red chillies and curry leaves. Fry them lightly and pour over the curry.

METHOD

1. Add salt to the flour, sprinkle some water over it and mix lightly with the tip of your fingers till it resembles breadcrumbs. Take a small aluminium bowl and pack this mixture alternately with grated coconut. Cover with a lid and steam in a mould in the pressure cooker. You could also use a puttu maker, a cylindrical steel or aluminium tube with a perforated lid and base.

METHOD

1. Heat oil in a small wok. Splutter mustard seeds and add all the ingredients one by one. Fry lightly and mix with the steamed mixture. Add 1 tbsp of the chicken gravy and mix well. Transfer this mixture to a bowl.

2. To serve, lift the chicken from the gravy and carve out the pieces. Place the pieces around a flat dish. Invert the rice flour mixture from the mould and place in the middle. Pour the gravy on the chicken pieces and serve.

34. Simple Chicken Roast

This is an old and familiar favourite in many Malayali homes.

Serves: 8

INGREDIENTS

Chicken: 1 kg

Chilli powder: ½ tsp

Turmeric powder: ¼ tsp

Salt to taste

Onions, finely sliced: 2

Tomatoes, pureed with a drop of vinegar: 2

Chilli powder: ½ tsp

Pepper powder: ½ tsp

Water: 4 cups

METHOD

1. Marinate the chicken with chilli powder, turmeric powder and salt.

2. Heat oil in a heavy-bottomed pan and fry the whole chicken, turning it around until it is brown all over. Remove and set aside.

3. In the same pan, fry the sliced onions to a brown colour. Remove and add the tomato puree. Sauté well.

4. Make a paste of chilli and pepper powders and add to the pan. Sauté well till the oil starts separating. Add 4 cups of water.

5. Once the water starts boiling, add the fried chicken and fried onions. Allow the chicken to cook well, leaving at least 2 cups of gravy.

6. While serving, carve the chicken and pour the hot gravy on the chicken pieces. Serve hot.

35. Minced Meat-Stuffed Brinjal

A delicious and filling dish, this can be enjoyed on its own, with accompaniments, or even with a simple salad.

Serves: 8

INGREDIENTS

Brinjals, medium-sized: 6

Meat, minced: ½ kg

Oil: ½ cup

Onions, chopped: ½ cup

Green chilli, chopped: 1

Ginger, chopped: 2 tsp

Vinegar: 1 tbsp

Salt: 1 tsp

Peppercorns, crushed: 1 tsp

Cloves, powdered: ½ tsp

Cinnamon, powdered: ½ tsp

Cardamom, powdered: ¼ tsp

Mashed potato: ½ cup

Egg: 1

Breadcrumbs: ¼ cup

METHOD

1. Steam the brinjals with the stalk for about 5 minutes. Leave them to cool. Once they have cooled, cut each brinjal into 2, lengthwise. Scoop out half the pulp, retaining the shape of the brinjal. Keep the pulp aside.

2. Heat 2 tbsp oil in a pan. Sauté onions, green chillies and ginger. When the onions start to brown, add the meat, vinegar and salt.

3. Cover the pan and leave it to cook. Do not add water as there will be enough in the meat itself. Stir at intervals to avoid burning or sticking to the bottom. Once the mince is cooked, add crushed peppercorns, clove, cinnamon and cardamom powders. Mix well and remove from the flame.

4. After the minced meat has cooled sufficiently, add the mashed potato and the brinjal pulp. Mix well. Check if the salt is adequate. Keep aside.

5. In a separate bowl, whisk the egg until light and frothy. Using a pastry brush, lightly apply a thin layer of the beaten egg on the inside of the steamed brinjal. Then stuff the hollowed-out brinjal with the minced meat and potato-brinjal mixture.

6. Apply a thin layer of the beaten egg on the top of the stuffed brinjal. Sprinkle a thin layer of breadcrumbs on the top.

7. In a heavy-bottomed wok, heat some oil. Deep fry the stuffed brinjal with the breadcrumbed side downward. Fry in small batches. Use a slotted spoon to lift the brinjal out of the oil and allow the oil to drain. Serve hot.

36. Mixed Meat Grill

A simple dinner can be elevated into something special and scrumptious by grilling different meats and serving them on a large platter.

Serves: 20

INGREDIENTS

Beef: ½ kg

Pork: ½ kg

Chicken: ½ kg

Liver: ½ kg

Sausages: ½ kg

Capsicum: 3 (1 each of green, yellow and red)

Celery stalks: 3

Onions: 5 cups

Oil: ½ cup

Ginger paste: 2 tbsp

Garlic paste: 2 tbsp

Chilli powder: 2 tbsp

Pepper powder: 2 tbsp

Soy sauce: 2 tbsp

Tomato sauce: 2 tbsp

Worcestershire sauce: 2 tbsp

Salt to taste

METHOD

1. Slice the various meats into even sizes. Cut the onions, capsicum and celery into cubes. Heat a pan and sauté the vegetables. Keep them aside.

2. Prepare the marinade by mixing ginger and garlic pastes, pepper and chilli powders, soy sauce, tomato sauce and Worcestershire sauce. Marinate the meats separately for an hour.

3. Cook the meats separately. Drain off the meat pieces from the gravies and keep aside.

4. Heat oil in a pan and fry the meats separately to a light brown colour.

5. Mix all the gravies together in the pan. Cook till the gravy is thick and coats the back of a spoon. Now add all the sautéed meats and vegetables to the gravy and mix well. Serve hot.

37. Kuttanad Duck Curry

Kuttanad in Kerala is famous for its backwaters and the toddy shops that serve up local favourites. Kuttanad duck is a much-loved delicacy. These recipes for duck curries include a variety of dishes to suit all tastes and preferences and can be served with appams, puttu, idiyappams, rice or parottas.

Serves: 6

INGREDIENTS

Duck, cut into medium-sized pcs: 1 kg

Ginger, crushed: 1½

Garlic cloves, crushed: 15

Water: 2 cups

Salt to taste

Coconut oil: ½ cup

Shallots, crushed: 10

Green chillies, crushed: 10

Peppercorns, crushed: 2 tsp

Turmeric powder: ½ tsp

Thick coconut milk: 2 cups

Curry leaves: 1 sprig

Spice powder

Dry roast

Cinnamon: 2-inch pcs

Cloves: 4

Cardamoms: 4

Aniseed: 1 tsp

Star anise: 2

METHOD

1. Wash, clean and cut the meat into medium-sized pieces.

2. Cook with crushed ginger, garlic, water and salt to taste, till the pieces are soft and the gravy is thick.

3. Heat coconut oil in a pan. Sauté crushed shallots, green chillies, crushed pepper, turmeric powder, spice powder and curry leaves. Add coconut milk. Stir well and add salt to taste. Finally, add the duck pieces into the gravy and mix well. Serve hot.

38. Duck Fry with Gravy

Duck is a hot favourite in some homes and ours is no different. The goodness of coconut can be enjoyed in this gravy dish.

Serves: 6

INGREDIENTS

Duck: 750 g

Dry red chillies: 6

Peppercorns: 1 tsp

Cumin seeds: ½ tsp

Mustard seeds: ½ tsp

Turmeric powder: ¼ tsp

Cinnamon: 1-inch piece

Cloves: 6

Oil: ¼ cup

Shallots, ground to a paste: 18

Ginger, ground into a paste:
1-inch piece

Garlic, ground into a paste: 6

Vinegar: 1 tbsp

Salt to taste

Coconut, grated, fried brown,
and ground: 1 cup

METHOD

1. Wash, clean and cut the duck into fairly big pieces.

2. Roast dry red chillies, peppercorns, cumin seeds, mustard seeds, cinnamon, cloves and turmeric powder. Grind these to a paste.

3. Heat oil in a wok and sauté the shallot paste, followed by ginger and garlic pastes. Sauté well. When done, add the ground paste (see Step 2) and sauté again.

4. Add the duck pieces and fry until they are coated with the gravy. Add vinegar, salt and hot water and let the meat cook. After it is cooked, add the ground coconut paste with a little water. When it starts to boil and the oil surfaces on top, remove from the flame.

39. Special Duck Curry

Any connoisseur's delight, this curry brings out the flavours of the spices and coconut.

Serves: 8

INGREDIENTS

Duck: 1 kg

Coriander powder: 3 tsp

Peppercorns: 1 tbsp

Aniseed: 1 tsp

Turmeric powder: ½ tsp

Cinnamon: 1-inch piece

Star anise: 2

Cloves: 2

Cardamom pods: 3

Oil: ½ cup

Onions: 5 cups

Ginger, finely sliced: 1-inch piece

Garlic pod, sliced: 1

Green chillies, slit: 3

Vinegar: 1 tbsp

Salt to taste

Coconut, grated, to extract milk: 1½

1st extract: 1 cup

2nd extract: 3 cups

METHOD

1. Wash, clean and cut the duck into 10 pieces.

2. Lightly roast the peppercorns, aniseed, cinnamon, star anise, cloves, cardamom and powder. Mix the coriander and turmeric powders. Make a paste of the powdered ingredients with a little water. Set aside.

3. Heat a heavy-bottomed pan with oil. Sauté the onions, ginger, garlic and green chillies. Add the paste and continue frying over a low flame.

4. Add the duck pieces, vinegar and salt and cook for about 5 minutes. Then pour the 2nd extract of coconut milk. Cover and cook the duck.

5. When the duck is done, add the 1st extract of coconut milk. Remove from fire as soon as it starts to boil.

For tempering

Oil: ¼ cup

Mustard seeds: ½ tsp

Shallots: 1 tbsp

Curry leaves: 2 sprigs

Medium-sized tomato, sliced into 6 pcs

6. In a separate pan, heat oil and ghee and throw in the mustard seeds. When it splutters, add shallots, curry leaves and tomato slices.

7. Lightly fry and pour this over the duck curry. Serve hot.

40. Duck Piralen

A Kerala-style dish cooked and simmered in a spicy gravy, this goes well with hoppers, varieties of breads and rice.

Serves: 6

INGREDIENTS

Duck: 1 kg

Coriander seeds: 3 tbsp

Kashmiri chillies, whole: 15

Turmeric powder: 1 tsp

Cinnamon: 1-inch piece

Cloves: 2

Cardamoms: 3

Aniseed: 1 tsp

Vinegar: 1 tbsp

Salt to taste

For tempering

Oil: 2 tbsp

Mustard seeds: 1 tsp

Cumin seeds: ½ tsp

Ginger, sliced: 1-inch piece

Garlic cloves: 15

Curry leaves: 1 sprig

Shallots: 1 cup

Peppercorns, crushed: 1 tbsp

METHOD

1. Wash, clean and slice the duck into medium-sized pieces.

2. Heat oil in a wok and lightly fry the coriander seeds and red chillies, and remove them. Save the oil for tempering.

3. Grind turmeric powder, cinnamon, cardamom, cloves and aniseed along with the fried coriander seeds and red chillies.

4. Mix the duck pieces with this ground paste. Add the vinegar and salt to taste. Sprinkle some water and cook in a pressure cooker on high flame till the first whistle. Reduce the flame to medium and cook for 2 more whistles. Once the duck is cooked well and the gravy is thick, remove from the flame.

For tempering

1. Heat the saved oil. Add mustard and cumin seeds first and then ginger, garlic and curry leaves. Sauté well till the garlic turns slightly brown. Add shallots and keep stirring. Add the duck with the gravy and mix well. Finally, add the crushed pepper and remove from the fire. Serve hot.

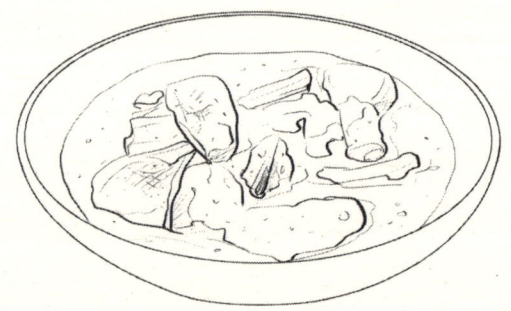

41. Backwater Duck Piralen

The flavour and aroma of the spices add to the taste of this special type of duck found in the backwaters of Kerala.

Serves: 6

INGREDIENTS

Duck: 1 kg

Onions, sliced: 2

Green chillies, slit: 4

Ginger, sliced: 1-inch piece

Oil: ¼ cup

Coriander powder: 3 tsp

Chilli powder: 2 tsp

Turmeric powder: 1 tsp

Pepper powder: 1 tsp

Aniseed: 1 tsp

Spice powder: 1 tsp

Garlic cloves: 5

Shallots: 5

Vinegar: 1 tbsp

Salt to taste

METHOD

1. Wash, clean and cut the duck into medium-sized pieces. Grind the coriander, chilli, turmeric and pepper powders, along with aniseed, spice powder, garlic cloves and shallots. Set aside the ground paste.

2. Heat oil in a heavy-bottomed vessel. Sauté the onions, green chillies and ginger. Lower the flame and add the ground ingredients. Keep stirring till the paste turns a rich brown. Add the duck, vinegar and salt, and mix well. Continue frying on a low flame till all the ingredients are blended and the meat is cooked. Serve hot.

Seafood Dishes

1. Fish Fry
2. Fish Molee
3. Red Fish Curry
4. Fish with Grated Coconut
5. Roast Fish
6. Fish Cooked in Banana Leaves
7. Masala Pomfret
8. Meen Kolembu
9. Vembanad Karimeen
10. Goan Fish Curry
11. Malabar Fish Curry
12. Alleppey Fish Curry with Mangoes
13. Sardines Vattichathu
14. Sardines Cooked in Pressure Cooker
15. Fish Roe Cakes
16. Fish Cutlets
17. Prawn Ularth
18. Lobster Fry
19. Prawn Mappas
20. Prawns in Lemon Garlic Sauce
21. Prawn Batter Fry
22. Dry Prawn and Mango Curry
23. Baked Fish
24. Chilli Fish
25. Masala Mussels
26. Crab Ularth
27. Anchovy (Natholi) Crispies

1. Fish Fry

The aromas of fried fish emanate from most homes in Kerala.

Yields: 6

INGREDIENTS

Fish: ½ kg

Chilli powder: 1 tbsp

Turmeric powder: ¼ tsp

Pepper powder: ½ tsp

Ginger: 1-inch piece

Garlic cloves: 6

Salt to taste

Oil for frying (enough to deep fry)

METHOD

1. Clean the fish well in salt water and slice it into pieces.

2. Grind chilli, turmeric and pepper powders along with ginger and garlic. Add salt to taste. Marinate the fish with this paste and let it rest for some time.

3. Add some oil into a heavy-bottomed skillet. Deep fry the fish on both sides, turning it gently. It can be shallow-fried too. Serve hot with vinegary onion rings or a fresh salad.

2. Fish Molee

A mildly spiced creamy curry with coconut milk; this recipe dates back to the time when the Portuguese first came to the Kerala coast.

Serves: 10

INGREDIENTS

Fish pcs: 500 g

Oil: ¼ cup

Onion, sliced: 1 cup

Ginger, crushed: 1 tsp

Garlic, crushed: 1 tsp

Green chillies, partially slit: 6

Peppercorns, crushed: ½ tsp

Curry leaves: 2 sprigs

1st extract of coconut milk from freshly grated coconut: ½ cup, thick

2nd extract of coconut milk: 2 cups

Salt to taste

Tomato, quartered: 1 big

METHOD

1. Clean the fish well in salt water.

2. Heat some oil in a pan. Sauté onion, ginger, garlic, green chillies, peppercorns and curry leaves. Transfer the sautéed ingredients to an earthen pot or a deep pan. Add the 2nd extract of coconut milk and allow this to simmer. Add the fish pieces and salt. Cover the pan and cook on low flame until the gravy thickens. Add tomato and the 1st extract of coconut milk. Do not stir with a spoon or ladle, instead take the pan off the heat, hold carefully with both hands and gently rotate or shake carefully so that the contents are well mixed. This process will prevent the fish from breaking. Continue to cook over low flame till the fish is fully cooked.

3. Red Fish Curry

A very popular spicy fish curry that is made regularly in Syrian-Christian homes, especially in the central Kerala region. This curry is also an integral part of the Syrian-Christian marriage feast. It is usually made in a chatti (earthenware pan) and the unique tangy flavour comes from the kokum that is added to the curry.

Serves: 6

INGREDIENTS

Fish pcs: 500 g

Chilli powder: 5 tsp

Turmeric powder: ½ tsp

Shallot: 1

Ginger, sliced: 2 tsp

Garlic cloves: 12

Oil: ½ cup

Mustard seeds: 1 tsp

Fenugreek seeds: ½ tsp

Sliced shallots: 4 tsp

Curry leaves: 4 sprigs

Kokum, washed and soaked in water: 3 pcs

Water: 2 cups

Salt to taste

METHOD

1. Clean the fish pieces well in salt water. Grind the chilli and turmeric powders along with the shallot into a paste. Take half the quantity of ginger and garlic. Grind this into a paste. Slice the rest of the ginger and garlic into thin pieces.

2. Heat oil in a pan or an earthen pot. Splutter mustard and fenugreek seeds. Add the sliced shallots, ginger, garlic and curry leaves. When this turns light brown, drain from the oil and keep aside. In the same pan, stir in the ground paste and add the sliced ginger and garlic. Sauté well and keep adding teaspoons of the soaked kokum water. Continue stirring on low flame until the raw smell goes.

3. Transfer the sautéed ingredients and the soaked kokum with water to a terracotta (preferable) or any heavy-bottomed vessel. Add water, and once it boils, add the fish pieces and salt. Cook with the lid half covered until the gravy is fairly thick.

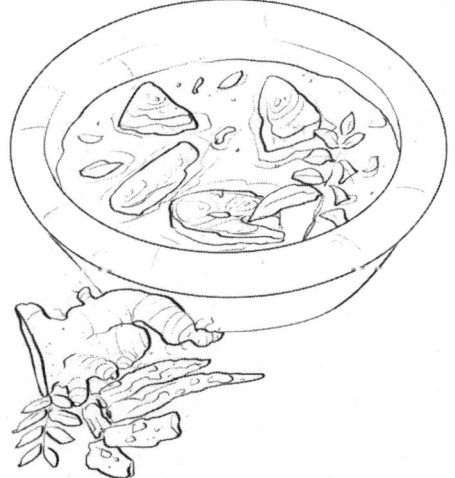

4. Fish with Grated Coconut

This is a much-loved dish in Kerala, resembling a thoran, cooked with freshly grated coconut and kokum. You could use any small fish, such as anchovies which are the most popular, smaller-sized mackerel cut into chunks or small cubes of bigger fish (preferably boneless). This dish is light and full of flavour.

Serves: 8

INGREDIENTS

Fish, cut into small cubes: 500 g

Coconut, grated: 2 cups

Shallots: 10

Ginger: 1-inch piece

Garlic cloves: 6

Green chillies, sliced: 4–5

Turmeric powder: ½ tsp

Curry leaves: 3

Salt to taste

Kokum, washed and soaked in water: 3

Water: 1 cup

Oil (preferably coconut): 2 tbsp

METHOD

1. Clean the fish in salt water. Coarsely crush coconut, shallots, ginger, garlic and green chillies using a mortar and pestle or on a grinding stone. If using a mixer-grinder or food processor, just pulse the mix once or twice till the ingredients are mixed but not ground. Add turmeric powder. Mix the fish with the crushed ingredients and curry leaves. Add salt to taste.

2. Put the mixture in a shallow pan or in an earthen pot. Add kokum and one cup of water to cook the fish. Bring to a boil and then lower the flame and allow the mixture to dry out, gently stirring or shaking the pan occasionally so that it does not stick to the bottom. Once the fish is cooked and looks dry but is still moist, remove from flame and drizzle a couple of teaspoons of coconut oil.

5. Roast Fish

This is a very traditional and much-loved fish preparation in Kerala, cooked and served on a wilted banana leaf.

Serves: 4

INGREDIENTS

Pomfret, pearl spot or any other similar fish, cleaned and scored, preferably whole: 500 g

Chilli powder: 1 tsp

Pepper powder: ½ tsp

Turmeric powder: ¼ tsp

Shallots: 3

Ginger, sliced: ½ inch piece

Garlic cloves: 4

Vinegar: 1 tbsp

Salt to taste

Oil: ¼ cup

Onions, thinly sliced: 1 cup

Ginger, thinly sliced: 1 tsp

Garlic, thinly sliced: 1 tsp

Curry leaves: 2 sprigs

Coconut milk extracted from 1 cup grated coconut: ¾ cup

METHOD

1. Grind chilli, pepper and turmeric powders along with garlic and shallots in 1 tbsp vinegar. Add some salt and marinate the fish for 30 minutes.

2. Heat oil in a skillet. Sauté sliced onions, ginger, garlic and curry leaves. Before the ingredients change colour, add the fish. Fry the fish on medium flame, gently turning it over till the marinade is well roasted, then ladle the onions and oil over the fish. Add coconut milk and swirl the pan around to mix the ingredients. Allow the curry to simmer over medium flame. Keep ladling the gravy over the fish. The fish may be turned over once if needed, but be careful as it may break. When the gravy thickens, remove from the flame.

3. Wilt a section of a banana leaf and spread it in a wide and deep dish. Place the fish on the leaf, pour the gravy over it and serve hot.

6. Fish Cooked in Banana Leaves

This is another version of meen pollichathu, in which the cooked fish is baked in banana leaf parcels.

Serves: 4

INGREDIENTS

Fish slices: 500 g

Turmeric powder: ½ tsp

Chilli powder: 1 tsp

Salt to taste

Onions, large, chopped: 3

Ginger, julienned: 1-inch piece

Garlic cloves: 1 whole pod

Green chillies, slit: 3

Tomatoes, chopped: 1½ cups

Curry leaves: 3 sprigs

Oil: ¾ cup

Thick coconut milk extracted from half a coconut: 1 cup

METHOD

1. Make a paste of chilli and turmeric powders, add salt to taste and marinate the fish pieces. Heat a pan with half the quantity of oil. Lightly fry the fish pieces. Set aside.

2. Into the remaining oil, add chopped onions, ginger, garlic, green chillies and curry leaves. Sauté until light brown. Add the tomatoes and stir until they are well cooked. Finally, add the coconut milk. Ladle the fish pieces into the gravy. Allow the curry to simmer till the gravy coats the fish. Remove from flame.

3. Wilt a banana leaf by passing it back and forth over a low flame. Cut the leaf into small pieces, each piece large enough to be wrapped around a piece of fish. Place a piece on a leaf and fold it into a small parcel. Arrange all the pieces in a baking dish and bake in a preheated oven at 350°F for 15 minutes.

7. Masala Pomfret

Black pepper, red chilli powder and green chillies combine with the sharp tang of lime in the marinade; the stuffing adds another layer of flavour.

Serves: 4

INGREDIENTS
Pomfret: 500 g

For the marinade
Shallots: 5

Ginger: ½ inch piece

Garlic cloves: 4

Chilli powder: 1 tsp

Turmeric powder: ¼ tsp

Pepper powder: ½ tsp

Fenugreek seeds: ¼ tsp

Cumin seeds: ¼ tsp

Mustard seeds: ¼ tsp

Lime juice: 1 tbsp

Salt: 1 tsp

For the stuffing
Oil: ½ cup

Onion, chopped: ½ cup

Ginger, chopped: ½ tsp

Green chillies, chopped: 1 tsp

Tomatoes, chopped: ½ cup

Sugar: ⅛ tsp

Salt to taste: ½ tsp

White of 1 egg, beaten stiff

METHOD

1. Clean the whole fish in salt water. Score both sides lightly. Make a slit on one side of the fish from the side of the mouth to the beginning of the tail.

2. Grind all the items listed under the marinade together. Coat this on the fish and set it aside for 1 hour.

3. Heat half the oil in a heavy-bottomed pan. Lightly fry the onions, ginger and green chillies until golden brown. Add tomatoes. Sauté well until they are dry. Add sugar and salt to this mixture, and stuff it into the slit part, spreading evenly. Beat the egg white stiff and seal the side with it.

4. Heat the remaining oil in a skillet. Fry the fish on both sides. Serve hot.

8. Meen Kolembu

Kolembu or kuzhambu means curry in Tamil. The addition of tamarind gives this curry its distinctive flavour.

Serves: 6

INGREDIENTS

Fish, cut into medium-sized pcs: 500 g

Chilli powder: 1 tsp

Cumin seeds, roasted: ¾ tsp

Pepper seeds: ½ tsp

Turmeric powder: ½ tsp

Ginger: A small piece

Garlic cloves: 5

Oil: ¼ cup

Shallots, sliced: 4

Green chillies, slit: 2

Curry leaves: 2 sprigs

Tomato puree: 1 medium-sized tomato

Tamarind extract: Approx. ⅓ cup (if concentrate, use 2 tsp)

Salt to taste

METHOD

1. Clean the fish pieces and keep them aside. Grind chilli powder, cumin seeds, pepper, turmeric powder, ginger and garlic to a paste.

2. Heat oil in a terracotta pot, sauté shallots, green chillies and curry leaves. Add the ground paste and fry well. Add tomato and sauté again.

3. Strain the tamarind water and mix with the sautéed ingredients. Add salt to taste. Finally, add the fish. Mix well. Simmer till the fish is cooked and the gravy is thick.

9. Vembanad Karimeen

Karimeen or Pearl Spot is Kerala's favourite fish. It can be found in many lakes, but the ones from Vembanad Lake are considered by connoisseurs to be the tastiest.

Serves: 3

INGREDIENTS

Karimeen: 500 g

Chilli powder: 1 tsp

Turmeric powder: ¼ tsp

Ginger paste: ½ tbsp

Garlic paste: ½ tbsp

Salt to taste

Oil: ¼ cup

Mustard seeds: 1 tsp

Shallots: 2 cups

Ginger paste: 1 tsp

Garlic paste: 1 tsp

Green chillies, slit: 2

Tomatoes, medium-sized, chopped: 2

Chilli powder: 1 tsp

Turmeric powder: ½ tsp

Aniseed powder: ½ tsp

Salt to taste

Curry leaves: 2 sprigs

METHOD

1. Clean the fish and make gashes on it. Moisten chilli powder, turmeric powder, 1 tbsp ginger and garlic paste with a little water and make a marinade. Coat the fish and set aside for 30 minutes.

2. Heat a pan with oil and lightly fry the fish. Remove the fish. In the same pan, splutter mustard seeds. Add shallots, followed by 2 tsp ginger and garlic pastes and green chillies. Sauté well. Add the tomatoes. Moisten chilli, turmeric and aniseed powders with a little water and add to the sautéed ingredients. Continue to sauté till oil separates. Now, place the fish gently on the pan and coat it with the sautéed ingredients. Serve hot.

10. Goan Fish Curry

Goan fish curry is not only a regional staple but is popular all over India.
This tangy and spicy dish is usually served with steamed rice.

Serves: 6

INGREDIENTS

Fish: 500 g

Kokum, washed and soaked in water: 4

Coriander powder: 2 tsp

Chilli powder: 1 tsp

Turmeric powder: ½ tsp

Cumin seeds: ½ tsp

Garlic cloves: 1 pod

Green chillies: 3

Coconut, grated: ½ cup

Oil: ½ cup

Shallots: ¼ cup

Ginger, sliced: 1 tsp

Green chillies, slit: 3

1st extract of coconut milk: 2 cups

2nd extract of coconut milk: 1 cup

Salt: 1 tsp

METHOD

1. Cut the fish into large cubes, clean in salt water and keep aside. Wash the kokum and soak in ½ cup water. Allow it to soften, then squeeze and extract the water. Strain and keep aside.

2. Grind coriander powder, chilli powder, turmeric powder, cumin seeds, garlic, green chillies and grated coconut together into a fine paste.

3. Heat oil in a heavy-bottomed pan. Add shallots, ginger and green chillies, and sauté well. Add the ground paste, and sauté well till the oil separates. Add the fish and mix well. Add the kokum extract and salt to taste. Mix in the 2nd extract of coconut milk. When the fish is cooked and gravy is thick, add the 1st extract of coconut milk. Do not stir, but gently swirl the pan. Once the curry begins to boil, remove from the fire. Serve hot.

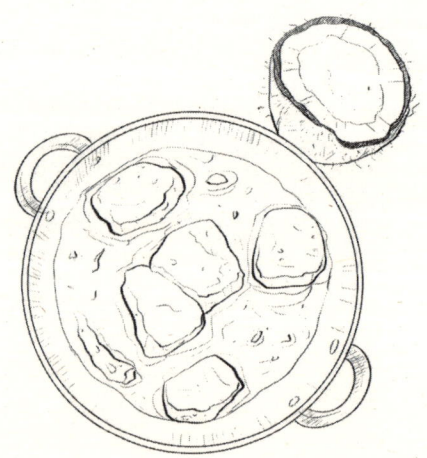

11. Malabar Fish Curry

The rich coconut milk gravy makes this a crowd-pleaser. It is usually served with steamed rice,
but we used to enjoy it with freshly baked bread at our family gatherings.

Serves: 6

INGREDIENTS

Fish cubes: 500 g

Coconut oil: ¾ cup

Mustard seeds: 1 tsp

Fenugreek seeds: ½ tsp

Curry leaves: 2

Onions, chopped: 1 cup

Shallots, sliced: ¼ cup

Ginger, sliced: 1 tbsp

Garlic, sliced: 1 tbsp

Chilli powder: 1½ tbsp

Turmeric powder: 1 tsp

Coriander powder: 1 tbsp

Puree extracted from a
gooseberry-sized piece of
tamarind: ½ cup

Coconut milk, thick (extracted
from 1 coconut): 3 cups

Salt to taste

METHOD

1. Clean the fish in salt water.

2. Heat oil in a heavy-bottomed vessel or an earthen pot. Splutter mustard seeds and add fenugreek seeds followed by curry leaves. Add shallots, ginger and garlic, and sauté well. Make a paste of chilli, turmeric and coriander powders with a little water. Stir this paste into the sautéed ingredients, and lightly fry till the oil starts separating. Add the fish pieces and salt to taste. Add tamarind extract and coconut milk.

3. Simmer on a low flame till the fish is cooked. Do not stir, but gently swirl the pan. Once the gravy is thick, remove from the flame.

12. Alleppey Fish Curry with Mangoes

Alleppey, with its huge network of canals, is known as the Venice of the East. It is also home to this well-known curry, which owes its tangy flavour to the generous use of raw mangoes.

Serves: 6

INGREDIENTS

Fish pcs: 500 g

Chilli powder: 2 tsp

Coriander powder: 1 tsp

Turmeric powder: ½ tsp

A little water

Oil: ¼ cup

Mustard seeds: ½ tsp

Onion, sliced: 1 cup

Shallots, sliced: 1½ cups

Ginger, sliced: 1 tsp

Green chillies, slit: 5

Curry leaves: 2 sprigs

Raw mango, sliced: 1 cup

1st milk extracted from 1 grated coconut: 1 cup

2nd milk extracted from the same grated coconut: 2½ cups

METHOD

1. Clean the fish in salt water. Cut into 2-inch cubes.

2. Moisten chilli, coriander and turmeric powders in a little water and grind to a paste.

3. In a terracotta pot or a heavy-bottomed pan, heat the oil and splutter mustard seeds.

4. Add onions, shallots, ginger, green chillies and curry leaves. Once sautéed, add the ground paste. Keep sautéing till the oil separates.

5. Add the 2nd extract of coconut milk and allow to boil. Add the raw mango and salt. Once the mango is half-cooked, add the fish pieces. After it is cooked, add the 1st extract of coconut milk.

6. When the thick coconut milk starts to bubble, stir well and remove from flame. Serve hot.

13. Sardines Vattichathu

Sardines are called matthi in Kerala, and are not only delicious but extremely healthy as they are rich in Omega-3.

Serves: 6

INGREDIENTS

Sardines: 500 g

Red chillies: 10

Fenugreek seeds: ¼ tsp

Peppercorns: 8

Turmeric powder: ½ tsp

Shallots: ½ cup

Garlic cloves: ½ tbsp

Curry leaves: 2 sprigs

Coconut oil: ½ cup

Kokum, washed and soaked in ½ cup water: 3

Salt to taste

Water: ½ cup

METHOD

1. Clean the sardines in salt water. Make a slit on the side and remove the insides.

2. Coarsely grind red chillies, fenugreek seeds, peppercorns, turmeric powder, shallots, garlic cloves and curry leaves.

3. Mix the ground ingredients with some coconut oil, kokum (softened in water) and salt. Grease an earthen vessel with coconut oil and layer the fish and the ground ingredients alternately, finishing with a layer of ground ingredients. Add water and cook the fish and bring to a boil. Simmer over low flame till it is dry. Serve hot.

14. Sardines Cooked in Pressure Cooker

Pressure cooking fish might seem like an odd thing to do. But try this unusual
recipe using fresh sardines and crushed spices.

Serves: 6

INGREDIENTS

Sardines: 500 g

Ginger, sliced: 1 tsp

Garlic cloves, sliced: 2 tsp

Green chillies, slit: 5

Onion, finely chopped: ½ cup

Chilli powder: 1 tsp

Lime juice: 2 tbsp

Salt: 1 tsp

Oil: ¼ cup

METHOD

1. Clean the sardines in salt water. Make gashes on either side of the fish.

2. Place ginger, garlic, green chillies, onion, chilli powder, lime juice and salt in a mortar and pestle and crush lightly. Add oil and mix again.

3. Put half the crushed ingredients in a pressure cooker, and then place a layer of sardines. Use the remaining crushed ingredients to cover the fish. Cover the pressure cooker. After the first whistle, lower the flame and leave to cook for 15 minutes. After opening the pressure cooker, cook on a low flame till it is dry.

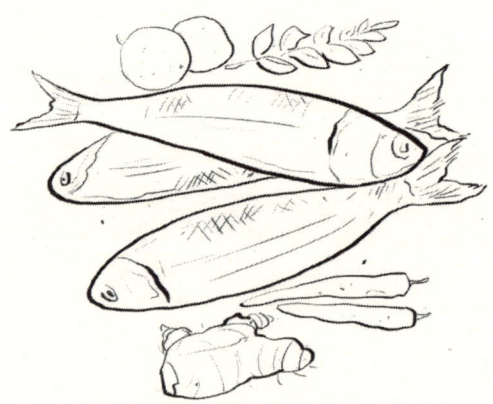

15. Fish Roe Cakes

Fish eggs, also known as roe, are high in Omega-3 fatty acids and are a rich source of Vitamin B12. These easy-to-make pancakes are an appetizing snack.

Yields: 3

INGREDIENTS

Fish roe, boiled with salt, turmeric powder and vinegar, skin removed and crumbled into small pcs: 1 cup

Onion, finely chopped: ¼ cup

Green chillies, finely chopped: 1 tbsp

Ginger, finely chopped: 1 tbsp

Coconut, grated: 2 tbsp

Pepper, coarsely powdered: 2 pinches

Salt to taste

Eggs: 2

Oil for frying

METHOD

1. Mix all the ingredients together with one egg. Add the other egg and mix again. Smear some oil on a hot frying pan. Ladle out a spoonful of the mixture to form pancakes. Cook on both sides.

Note: Apply oil to the pan before each pancake is made.

16. Fish Cutlets

Cutlets are popular in Kerala, Goa and West Bengal. Though freshly fried cutlets are best,
they also freeze well and are a handy snack.

Yields: 10

INGREDIENTS

Fish pcs: 500 g

Vinegar: 1 tbsp

Salt: 1 tsp

Potato: 2 cups

Oil: ½ cup

Onion, chopped: ½ cup

Ginger, chopped: 1 tsp

Green chillies, chopped: 2 tsp

Curry leaves, chopped: ½ tsp

Mint leaves, chopped: 1 tbsp

Pepper, crushed: ½ tsp

Egg yolk, beaten: 1

Egg white, whisked: 1

Breadcrumbs: 1 cup

METHOD

1. Clean the fish in salt water. Boil it in 1 cup water, vinegar and 1 tsp salt. Once cooked, remove the bones. Crumble the fish and keep aside.

2. Cook potatoes in water and salt. Mash and set aside. Heat 2 tbsp oil in a pan. Sauté the chopped onions, ginger, green chillies and curry leaves. Add the fish. Sprinkle crushed pepper and mix well. Remove from flame.

3. Add the mashed potato and beaten egg yolk. Taste the mixture and if needed, add more salt and pepper. Divide this mixture into 16 equal-sized balls. Then, flatten each ball into an oval-shaped cutlet.

4. Beat the egg white well. In another bowl, place the breadcrumbs. Dip each cutlet first in the beaten egg white and then roll in the breadcrumbs. Keep this aside.

5. Heat some oil in a wok. Fry the cutlets in batches of two until golden brown. Remove them with a slotted spoon and completely drain out the oil. Serve hot.

17. Prawn Ularth

Ularth is a Malayalam word that means to slow-cook and roast with a blend of spices.

Serves: 8

INGREDIENTS

Prawns: 1 kg

Ginger, sliced: 1 tbsp

Garlic cloves: 1 small pod

Turmeric powder: ½ tsp

Coriander powder: 1 tsp

Chilli powder: 2 tsp

Peppercorns, crushed: 1 tsp

Kokum: 3 pcs

Curry leaves: 4

Coconut, cut into small bits: ¼ cup

Salt: 1 tsp

Coconut oil: ¼ cup

Mustard seeds: 1 tsp

Fenugreek seeds: ¼ tsp

Dry red chillies, broken: 2

METHOD

1. Shell and devein the prawns. Wash well and set aside. Wash the kokum and leave to soak in ½ cup water.

2. In a terracotta vessel, mix prawns with all the ingredients. Add the extract from kokum along with curry leaves and salt. Cover the vessel with a lid and cook on medium flame for about 8 to 10 minutes. In a separate pan, prepare the seasoning.

3. Heat oil and splutter mustard seeds. Add fenugreek, red chillies, shallots and curry leaves. Lightly fry. Add the cooked prawns. Stir fry the prawns till they are coated with the sautéed ingredients. Remove from fire and serve hot.

18. Lobster Fry

Lobsters are commonly served boiled or steamed in their shell. This special,
personalized recipe gives it a spicy, delicious twist.

Serves: 4

INGREDIENTS

Lobsters: 6

Shallots: 8

Garlic cloves: 10

Chilli powder: ¾ tbsp

Turmeric powder: ¼ tsp

Nutmeg powder: ¼ tsp

Juice of 1 lime

Salt to taste

Skewers: 6

Rice flour: A couple of heaped
tsp, enough to coat the
lobsters lightly

METHOD

1. Clean the lobsters in salt water. Devein them carefully without breaking the
    shell. Retain only the head and tail. Thread the skewer carefully through the
    lobster to keep it intact.

2. Grind shallots, ginger, garlic and spice powders. Mix lime juice and add salt to
    taste. Rub the lobsters with this paste and marinate for 30 minutes. Just before
    frying, dust the lobsters with rice flour. Heat a griddle pan with some coconut
    oil. Place the lobsters on it and fry them, turning them at intervals so that they
    get evenly browned.

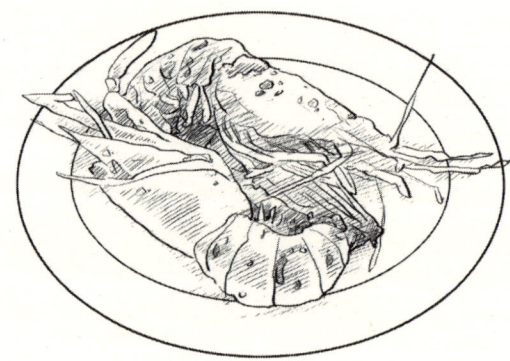

19. Prawn Mappas

Mappas is a coconut milk-based curry that appeals to everyone.

Serves: 6

INGREDIENTS

Prawns: 500 g

Chilli powder: 1 tsp

Coriander powder: 1 tbsp

Turmeric powder: ½ tsp

Peppercorns: 1 tsp

Shallots: 4

Oil: ¼ cup

Mustard seeds: 1 tsp

Fenugreek seeds: ⅛ tsp

Onion, sliced: 1 cup

Ginger, julienned: 1 tsp

Garlic cloves: 12

Green chillies, slit: 4

Kokum, washed and soaked in water: 4 pcs

1st extract of coconut milk: ½ cup

2nd extract of coconut milk: 2 cups

Salt to taste

METHOD

1. Wash the prawns well. Grind chilli powder, coriander powder, turmeric powder, peppercorns and shallots to a paste.

2. Heat oil in a pan and splutter mustard seeds. Add fenugreek seeds, followed by onions, ginger, garlic, green chillies and curry leaves. Sauté until the onions are light brown. Add the ground paste. Fry well till the oil separates.

3. Add the softened kokum to the sautéed ingredients. Transfer the ingredients to an earthen pot or a deep pan. Pour the 2nd extract of coconut milk, followed by salt to taste. Once the gravy begins to boil, add the prawns. Cook on medium heat. Allow the gravy to get thick. Finally, pour the 1st extract of coconut milk. When the gravy starts to boil, remove from flame.

20. Prawns in Lemon Garlic Sauce

This all-time favourite is easy to prepare. The butter, garlic and lime juice marinade keeps the prawns tender and juicy.

Serves: 8

INGREDIENTS

Prawns, cleaned and deveined with tail intact: 25

For the marinade

Ginger, ground: ½ tbsp

Garlic, ground: ½ tbsp

Pepper powder: ½ tbsp

Salt to taste

For the lemon garlic sauce

Butter: 2 tbsp

Garlic, ground: 1 tsp

Juice of a small lime

METHOD

1. Combine all the ingredients for the marinade in a bowl. Add the prawns and marinate for an hour.

2. Heat a griddle. Thread four or five marinated prawns on a skewer or a bamboo stick. Place these skewers on the heated griddle and keep turning while basting the prawns with the lemon-garlic sauce. Make sure the prawns are not overcooked and the pink colour is retained. Serve hot.

21. Prawn Batter Fry

A tried-and-tested recipe which will ensure that you get the consistency of the batter right and the prawns crispy every time.

Serves: 8

INGREDIENTS

Prawns with tail intact: 250 g

Salt and pepper to taste

Flour: 1½ cups

Cornflour: 1½ cups

Baking soda: Less than ¼ tsp

Salt to taste

Ice-cold soda water

A dash of lime juice

Oil for frying

METHOD

1. Devein the prawns. Wash well and pat them dry. Add salt and pepper. Keep aside for half an hour. Sieve the flour, cornflour and baking soda together. Add salt to taste.

2. Just before frying, add the iced soda water little by little to the sieved ingredients. Use a hand mixer to blend everything. Add enough iced soda water to make a fairly thick batter. The batter should not be watery.

3. Meanwhile, sprinkle some lime juice on the marinated prawns. Dip each prawn holding the tail in the batter. The batter should be coated well.

4. Heat oil in a wok. Fry the prawns in batches until golden brown. Remove them with a slotted spoon and completely drain off the oil.

Note: Do not add the lime juice early as it will make the prawns hard in texture. Once the batter is ready, fry the prawns immediately. These tasty morsels also make an excellent starter.

22. Dry Prawn and Mango Curry

Dried prawns combine well with the sharpness of raw mangoes, giving the curry a unique flavour.
This dish is popular all over Kerala and tastes best with steamed rice.

Serves: 8

INGREDIENTS

Prawns, dried: 1 cup

Oil: 1 tbsp

Coconut, grated: 1 cup

Coriander powder: 2 tsp

Chilli powder: 1 tsp

Turmeric powder: ½ tsp

Garlic cloves: 9

Green chillies, slit: 6

Ginger, chopped: 1 tbsp

Raw mango, sliced: 1 cup

Water: 1 cup

Salt to taste

For tempering

Oil: 1 tbsp

Mustard seeds: ½ tsp

Shallots, sliced: 1 tbsp

Dry red chillies: 3

Curry leaves: 2 sprigs

METHOD

1. Soak dried prawns in water for about 10 minutes. Rinse and pat them dry.

2. In a small wok, heat 1 tbsp oil. Add the prawns and sauté lightly till they turn light brown and remove from the flame. Gently crush the prawns using a mortar and pestle. Grind coconut to a smooth paste. Set this aside.

3. Grind coriander, chilli and turmeric powders along with garlic. In a terracotta pot or pan, mix the ground ingredients with the prawns. Add green chillies, ginger and mango and cook on a medium flame. When the mango pieces turn soft, add the coconut paste. Cook over a low flame till the curry thickens. Remove from flame.

4. Heat a wok with oil. Splutter mustard seeds, and add shallots, chillies and curry leaves. Sauté lightly. Pour the tempering over the curry. Mix well and serve.

23. Baked Fish

My mother loved taking a different approach to any dish. This one makes a perfect one-dish meal.

Serves: 4

INGREDIENTS

Boneless fish, cut into cubes: 500 g

Butter: 2 tbsp

Onion, finely chopped: 1

Garlic, sliced: 8 cloves

Ginger, sliced finely: ½ inch piece

Celery, diced: ¼ cup

Baby corn, diced: ¼ cup

Bell peppers, diced: ¼ cup

Coriander leaves, chopped: 1 tbsp

Butter: 2 tbsp

Flour: 1 tbsp

Milk: ¾ cup

Cheese, grated: ½ cup

Tomato slices for garnishing

METHOD

1. Melt butter in a pan. Sauté the chopped onion, garlic and ginger until golden in colour. Add the fish cubes. Mix gently. Add celery, baby corn, bell peppers and coriander leaves one by one. Mix again.

2. Gently move all the ingredients to one side of the pan. Add butter followed by flour. Stir well till the flour turns light brown.

3. Slowly pour milk. Keep stirring and add grated cheese along with salt and pepper.

4. Once the sauce becomes thick, mix in the fish and transfer to a greased baking dish. Garnish with tomato slices. Bake in an oven for 20 minutes at 300°F.

24. Chilli Fish

This delicious dish was served to us after my mother's visit to Hong Kong. Her version of chilli fish is much loved and greatly appreciated by all those who enjoy the exciting fusion of Indian and Chinese food.

Serves: 8

INGREDIENTS

Fish: 1 kg

Chilli powder: 2 tsp

Pepper powder: 1 tsp

Soy sauce: 1 tbsp

Oil: ½ cup

Onions, chopped: 2½ cups

Garlic cloves: 16

Dry red chillies: 20

Tomato, chopped: ½ cup

Tomato sauce: 1 tbsp

Fish stock: 1 cup

Vinegar: 1 tbsp

Salt: 1 tsp

Capsicum rings: ½ cup

Chopped celery: 1 tbsp

For the fish stock

Water: 3 cups

Fish: 250 g

Fish bones

METHOD

1. Clean the fish and set aside. To prepare the fish stock, take a large saucepan and pour 3 cups water. Add fish bones and 250 g fish. Cook on a low flame till the liquid is reduced to half. Strain and reserve the liquid which becomes the fish stock.

2. In a small bowl, mix chilli and pepper powders with soy sauce. Marinate the fish with this paste for about 30 minutes. Deseed dry red chillies and pound the skin coarsely.

3. Heat some oil in a large skillet and shallow fry the marinated fish. Drain and set aside. Strain the oil. Heat the strained oil in the same skillet and fry onions until golden brown.

4. Add the pounded chilli skin, chopped tomato and the tomato sauce. Keep frying until the oil separates. Pour the reserved fish stock, vinegar and salt into this sautéed mixture. Cook on a low flame until the sauce gets thick. Add the capsicum rings and celery. Stir well and remove from flame.

5. In a flat dish, place the fried fish and pour the hot sauce over it. Serve immediately.

25. Masala Mussels

Mussels or Kallumakkaya are a favourite, especially in north Kerala.
Using a terracotta pot enhances the flavour of this spicy dish.

Serves: 8

INGREDIENTS

Mussels, cleaned: 500 g

Ginger, crushed: 1-inch piece

Garlic, crushed: 5 cloves

Green chillies, slit: 2

Chilli powder: 1 heaped tsp

Turmeric powder: ¼ tsp

Salt to taste

Pepper powder: A dash

Oil: ¼ cup

Shallots, sliced: 5 to 6

Curry leaves: 3 sprigs

METHOD

1. In a terracotta pot, mix the mussels, ginger, garlic, green chillies, chilli powder, and turmeric powder together. Cook on a low flame. Sprinkle a little water. Add salt to taste. Once cooked, sprinkle a dash of pepper, mix well and remove from flame.

2. Heat oil in a wok. Add the sliced shallots and curry leaves. Finally, add the mussels. Sauté well and serve hot.

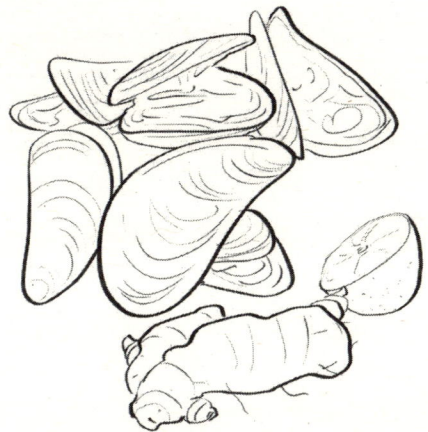

26. Crab Ularth

Ularth means to fry with a blend of roasted spices, and this dish is a crowd-pleaser.

Serves: 4

INGREDIENTS

Crabs, medium-sized: 6

Turmeric powder: ½ tsp

Salt to taste

Coconut oil: 3 tbsp

Mustard seeds: ¼ tsp

Curry leaves: A few sprigs

Shallots, cut into long slices: ½ cup

Dry red chillies, crushed: 1 tbsp

Garlic cloves, crushed (with skin): 1 tbsp

Peppercorns, crushed: ½ tbsp

Kokum: 1 or 2 pcs, soaked in ¼ cup water

METHOD

1. Put the crabs in boiling water with turmeric powder and salt, and cook for an hour.

2. When the shells turn orange, transfer the crabs to a bowl of cold water. This helps the crab flesh to firm up.

3. Remove the shell and take out the crab meat. There will be about 250 g crab meat.

4. Heat oil in a pan and splutter mustard seeds. Add curry leaves, shallots, dry red chillies, garlic cloves and crushed peppercorns. Add kokum and water. Lastly, stir in the crab meat, sauté until it is fried and crisp. Remove from flame and serve hot.

27. Anchovy (Natholi) Crispies

Anchovies are a versatile and tasty addition to salads and sauces. This recipe makes an addictive snack.

Serves: 8

INGREDIENTS

Anchovies, cleaned: 500 g

Chilli powder: 1 tbsp

Turmeric powder: ½ tsp

Ginger paste: 1 tbsp

Garlic paste: 1 tbsp

Salt to taste

Garnish

Coconut, grated: ½ cup

Green chillies, minced: 3

Shallots, minced: ½ cup

Coriander leaves, chopped: ½ cup

Juice of half a lime

Salt to taste

Oil

METHOD

1. Moisten chilli powder and turmeric powder with a little water to make the marinade. Mix with the ginger and garlic pastes. Add salt to taste. Marinate the anchovies with this paste and set aside for an hour.

METHOD

1. Heat some oil in a skillet. Fry the anchovies crisp. Drain off the excess oil and spread the anchovies on a plate. In a bowl, mix the ingredients listed under 'Garnish' and sprinkle over the fried anchovies. Serve.

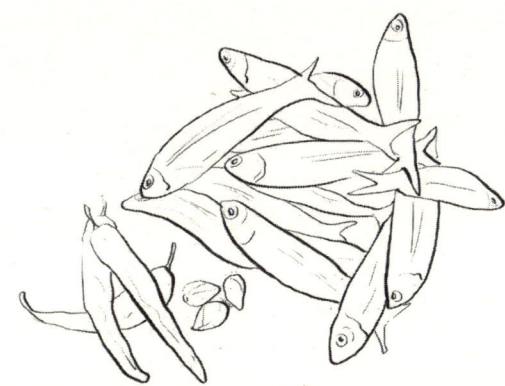

Vegetable Dishes

1. Parippu Curry
2. Sambar
3. Tomato Rasam
4. Mango Rasam
5. Kaalan
6. Avial
7. Olan
8. Erissery
9. Idichakka Thoran
10. Cheera Thoran
11. Kanji-payar Thoran
12. Pineapple Pachadi
13. Pachadi from Pickled Mango
14. Yellow Cucumber Pachadi
15. Mango Pachadi
16. Jackfruit Seed, Drumstick and Mango Curry
17. Theeyal
18. Ripe Mango Curry
19. Okra Curry
20. Masala Kadala
21. Kappa Purattiyathu
22. Mezhukkupuratti
23. Okra Fry
24. Kaya Varuthathu
25. Fried Bitter Gourd
26. Kachiya Moru
27. Spinach (Cheera) Cutlet
28. Mushroom Packets
29. Dal Kurma

1. Parippu Curry

Different from the way dal is prepared in north India, this is a simple, slightly bland curry made with ground coconut. It is traditionally served first with ghee on special occasions.

Serves: 15

INGREDIENTS

Dal (split green gram, cherupayar parippu): 1 cup

Water: 3 cups

Coconut, grated: 1 cup

Garlic cloves: 4

Chilli powder: ¼ tsp

Turmeric powder: ¼ tsp

Cumin seeds: ¼ tsp

Salt: ½ tsp

For tempering

Oil: 1 tbsp

Ghee: 1 tbsp

Mustard seeds: 1 tsp

Shallots, sliced: 2 tsp

Dry red chillies: 2

Curry leaves: 2 sprigs

METHOD

1. In a wok, lightly roast the dal. Cook the roasted dal in 3 cups water.

2. Grind chilli and turmeric powders with cumin seeds, garlic and grated coconut into a smooth paste.

3. Add it to the cooked dal. Add salt, and leave it to cook for a few minutes. When it boils, remove from flame.

4. Heat oil and ghee in a pan. Splutter mustard seeds, and add shallots, red chillies and curry leaves. Lightly fry and pour this over the curry. Serve hot.

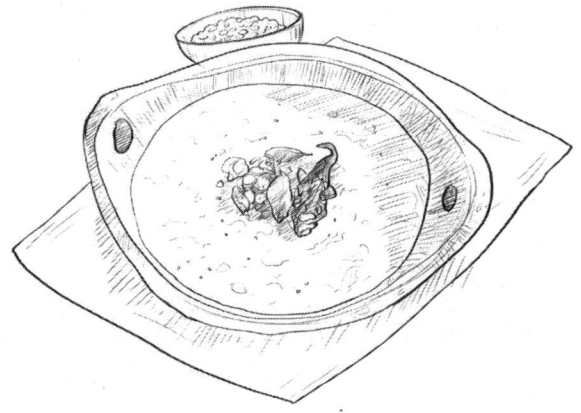

2. Sambar

There are as many recipes for sambar as there are cooks and kitchens. Some call for coconut to be added, some have a mix of vegetables, some use only pearl onions. Whatever recipe you follow, this is a versatile dish that goes well with rice, dosas, idlis, uthappams or vadas.

Serves: 15

INGREDIENTS

Toor dal (pigeon peas,): 1 cup

Mixed vegetables (brinjal, drumsticks, yellow cucumber [vellari], potato, onion): 250 g

Green chillies, slit: 4

Turmeric powder: 1 tsp

Sambar powder: 2 tbsp

Tamarind: 1 heaped tbsp

Water: 5½ cups

Salt: 1 tsp

For sambar powder

Oil: 1 tbsp

Coriander seeds, whole: 2 tbsp

Dry red chillies: 12

Fenugreek seeds: 1 tsp

Asafoetida powder: ½ tsp

For tempering

Oil: 1 tbsp

Mustard seeds: ½ tsp

Shallots, sliced: 1 tbsp

Dry red chilli, broken into two: 1

Curry leaves: 2 sprigs

Coriander leaves: 2 tbsp

METHOD

1. In a wok, heat oil. Start roasting the ingredients for sambar powder one by one. When all are done, powder them well. Store in an airtight container when cool, so that the aroma is not lost.

2. Cut the vegetables into 2-inch cubes. Wash and keep them aside.

3. Soak tamarind in ½ cup water for 20 minutes. Squeeze out the pulp, strain and keep this aside.

4. Wash the dal well. Cook it in 3 cups water and turmeric powder. Keep this aside.

5. In a separate pan, cook the vegetables, along with green chillies in 2 cups water.

6. When the vegetables are cooked, add the tamarind pulp, cooked dal, sambar powder and salt. Mix them well and leave to simmer on a low flame for about 10 minutes. Remove from the flame.

7. In a separate pan, make the tempering. Heat oil and splutter mustard seeds. Add shallots, dry red chilli and curry leaves. Lightly fry and pour this over the cooked dal and vegetables. Garnish with fresh coriander leaves. Serve hot.

Note: Sambar is usually made with tuvar dal. However, moong or masoor dal (cherupayar parippu or green gram) can also be used.

3. Tomato Rasam

A light, spicy broth with tomatoes, pepper, cumin seeds and garlic.

Serves: 6

INGREDIENTS

Toor dal (pigeon peas, tuvara parippu): ¼ cup

Tomatoes, thickly sliced: 4

Ginger, sliced: 1 tsp

Garlic cloves: 4

Coriander powder: ½ tsp

Chilli powder: ½ tsp

Cumin seeds: ½ tsp

Peppercorns: ¼ tsp

Asafoetida powder: ½ tsp

Lime juice: 1 tsp

Water: 4 cups

Salt: ½ tsp

For tempering

Oil: 1 tbsp

Mustard seeds: ½ tsp

Dry red chillies, broken into two: 2

Black gram: 1 tsp

Coriander leaves: 2 tbsp

METHOD

1. Cook the dal in 4 cups water until soft.

2. Crush garlic, ginger, cumin seeds and peppercorns along with coriander powder, chilli powder, tomatoes, asafoetida and salt. Add this to the dal.

3. When it boils, remove from flame and strain. Add lime juice.

4. For tempering, heat oil, splutter mustard seeds, and add the black gram dal, dry red chillies and coriander leaves. Fry this lightly and pour it over the rasam.

4. Mango Rasam

A variation of tomato rasam, this is slightly sweet and tangy with a hint of spice.

Serves: 6

INGREDIENTS

Ripe mango pcs, pureed:
½ cup

Toor dal (pigeon peas, tuvara parippu) cooked and mashed:
½ cup

Dry red chilli: 1

Peppercorns: 2 tsp

Garlic cloves, with skin: 12

Cumin seeds: ½ tsp

Curry leaves: 2 sprigs

Asafoetida as required

Salt to taste

Water: 2 cups

Coriander leaves: A bunch

Gingelly oil: 1 tbsp

Mustard seeds: 1 tsp

Fenugreek seeds: ½ tsp

Dry red chillies, quartered: 2

METHOD

1. Mix the mango puree and dal. Crush dry red chilli, peppercorns, garlic and cumin seeds and mix with the mango dal mixture along with curry leaves, asafoetida, salt and water. Boil this mixture. Strain and add coriander leaves.

2. Temper with mustard seeds, fenugreek seeds and dry red chillies fried in oil.

5. Kaalan

Made with plantains and coconut, with curd adding a creamy tang.

Serves: 10

INGREDIENTS

Ripe plantain, diced: 1 cup

Coconut, grated: 1 cup

Green chillies, slit: 6

Curd, beaten: 4 cups

Chilli powder: ½ tsp

Turmeric powder: ¼ tsp

Cumin seeds: ¼ tsp

Salt: ¼ tsp

Oil: 2 tbsp

Mustard seeds: 1 tsp

Fenugreek seeds: A pinch

Dry red chillies, broken into two: 3

Curry leaves: 2 sprigs

METHOD

1. Cook the plantain with chilli powder, turmeric powder, green chillies and salt in 1 cup water.

2. Grind coconut and cumin seeds to a paste. Add to the cooked plantain. Mix well and allow it to boil once.

3. Reduce the flame and add curd. Stir constantly so that it does not curdle. Remove from flame.

4. In a separate pan, heat oil, splutter mustard seeds, and add fenugreek seeds, dry red chillies and curry leaves. Fry lightly and pour over the curry.

Note: You can also use pineapple instead of plantain.

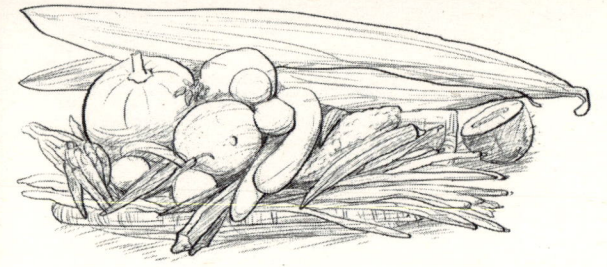

6. Avial

This mixed vegetable dish, all cut in roughly the same size and shape, is a staple in Kerala homes. It is also an integral part of the traditional sadya.

Serves: 10

INGREDIENTS

Mixed vegetables (drumsticks, yellow cucumber, string beans, brinjal, yam, raw banana and snake gourd): 500 g

Coconut, grated: 1 cup

Mango, raw, sliced: ½

Shallots: 4

Green chillies, slit: 8

Chilli powder: ½ tsp

Turmeric powder: ¼ tsp

Cumin seeds: ¼ tsp

Curry leaves: 2 sprigs

Coconut oil: 2 tbsp

Salt: 1 tsp

METHOD

1. Cut the vegetables into 2-inch-long pieces. Cook the harder vegetables such as yam, raw banana, etc., first with chilli and turmeric powders, green chillies and salt, in ½ cup water.

2. When they are half done, add the softer vegetables. Cook on a low flame without adding any more water.

3. Once the vegetables are cooked, add the raw mango and leave it to cook for a few more minutes.

4. Coarsely grind the grated coconut, shallots and cumin. Mix this with the cooked vegetables and allow to cook over a low flame.

5. Remove from the flame, add curry leaves and a few drops of coconut oil. Serve hot.

Note: You may substitute tamarind for mango.

7. Olan

This simple, stew-like curry gets its special flavour from coconut milk and coconut oil.

Serves: 10

INGREDIENTS

Red cowpeas (van payar):
½ cup

Ash gourd, diced: 2 cups

Green chillies, slit: 6

Curry leaves: 1 sprig

Thick coconut milk from the gratings of ¾ coconut: 1½ cups

Water: 2½ cups

Coconut oil: 1 tbsp

Salt to taste

METHOD

1. Pressure cook red cowpeas in 1½ cups water and set aside.

2. In a separate pan, cook the ash gourd in 1 cup water along with green chillies and salt.

3. Mix the red cowpeas with the ash gourd. Add coconut milk and curry leaves. Allow to simmer on a low flame for a few minutes. Remove from flame and drizzle coconut oil. Serve hot.

8. Erissery

Coconut is an important ingredient in any Kerala dish, and erissery is no exception. This is usually made with pumpkin, yam or plantain, to which some red cowpeas can be added.

Serves: 8

INGREDIENTS

Red cowpeas (van payar): ¼ cup

Pumpkin, finely chopped: 2 cups

Coconut, grated: ½ cup

Garlic cloves: 3

Chilli powder: ½ tsp

Turmeric powder: ½ tsp

Water: 2 cups

Salt: 1 tsp

For tempering

Coconut oil: 2 tbsp

Mustard seeds: 1 tsp

Shallots, sliced: 2 tbsp

Coconut, grated: 2 tbsp

Dry red chillies, broken into two: 2

Curry leaves: 2 sprigs

METHOD

1. Cook red cowpeas in 2 cups water. When done, add pumpkin and let it cook.

2. Coarsely grind coconut, turmeric and chilli powders along with garlic. Add this to the cooked pumpkin and red cowpea mix. Add salt and cook for a few minutes. Keep this aside.

3. In a separate pan, heat oil, splutter mustard seeds, and add sliced shallots, dry red chillies and curry leaves. Fry lightly, add grated coconut and sauté until golden brown. Remove from flame and pour this over the curry. Serve hot.

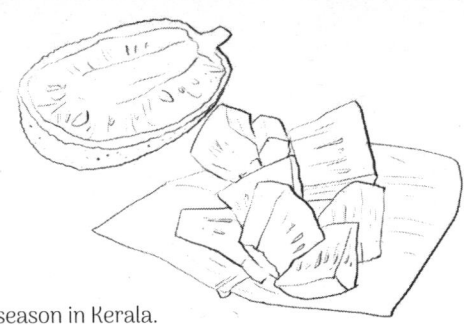

9. Idichakka Thoran

The idichakka signals the beginning of the much-awaited jackfruit season in Kerala.
Thoran is one among the variety of dishes that can be made out of the delicious fruit.

Serves: 8

INGREDIENTS

Tender jackfruit (idichakka), skinned and diced: 3 cups

Coconut, grated: 1 cup

Garlic cloves: 2

Chilli powder: ½ tsp

Turmeric powder: ¼ tsp

Cumin seeds: 1/2 tsp

Mustard seeds: 1 tsp

Dry red chillies: 2

Curry leaves: 1 sprig

Oil: 2 tbsp

METHOD

1. Cook the diced jackfruit in a steamer. Using a pestle and mortar, crush and shred the jackfruit. Keep this aside.

2. Coarsely grind coconut, chilli and turmeric powders, cumin seeds and garlic. Add the ground ingredients to the cooked jackfruit. Mix this well and set aside.

3. In a pan or wok, heat oil. Splutter mustard seeds and dry red chilli broken into two and curry leaves. Sauté lightly.

4. Then, add the cooked jackfruit and ground coconut mixture. Sauté this well till all the moisture dries out completely. Remove from the fire and serve hot.

Note: Cutting open the jackfruit, removing the pods and preparing them is a sticky, slippery process. Liberally applying coconut oil or any light cooking oil on your hands will help alleviate the stickiness. Alternatively, you could use food-grade gloves.

10. Cheera Thoran

More robust than spinach (palak), the red variety is more popular in south India and is very nutritious.

Serves: 6

INGREDIENTS

Spinach, finely chopped: 3 cups

Coconut, grated: 1 cup

Garlic cloves: 2

Green chilli, chopped: 1 tsp

Chilli powder: ¼ tsp

Turmeric powder: ¼ tsp

Mustard seeds: ½ tsp

Dry red chillies, broken into two: 2

Curry leaves: 3 sprigs

Oil: 2 tbsp

Salt: ¼ tsp

METHOD

1. Coarsely grind coconut, chilli and turmeric powders along with garlic. Keep this aside.

2. In a heavy-bottomed pan or wok, heat oil. Splutter mustard seeds and add dry red chillies and curry leaves. Fry lightly.

3. Add the chopped spinach and green chilli into the pan. Sprinkle a little water and add the salt. Cover the pan and leave it to cook for a few minutes. When the steam starts to rise, make a well in the middle of the spinach and put the ground coconut mixture into it. Use the remaining spinach to cover the mixture. Place the lid back and leave this to cook for a few minutes. Remove the lid and stir gently till all the water has been absorbed. Remove from the flame and serve hot.

Note: The same recipe can be used for cabbage and beans with carrots and raw papaya.

11. Kanji-payar Thoran

Thoran made with split green gram is delicious and is served as a traditional combination with kanji (rice gruel) .

Serves: 10

INGREDIENTS

Cherupayar (split green gram): 1 cup

Coconut, grated: 1 cup

Garlic cloves: 3

Green chilli, slit: 1

Turmeric powder: ¼ tsp

Cumin seeds: A pinch

Water: 3 cups

Salt: 1 tsp

For tempering

Oil: 2 tbsp

Mustard seeds: ½ tsp

Dry red chilli, broken into two: 1

Curry leaves: 3 sprigs

METHOD

1. Coarsely grind grated coconut, turmeric powder and cumin seeds along with garlic and green chilli. Set aside.

2. Wash the cherupayar and cook in 3 cups water. Before all the water gets absorbed into the cherupayar, add the ground ingredients. Leave this to cook for a few minutes. Add salt and mix it well.

3. In a separate pan, prepare the tempering. Heat oil, and splutter mustard seeds. Add dry red chilli and curry leaves. Fry lightly and stir into the cooked cherupayar.

12. Pineapple Pachadi

Both sweet and tangy with a hint of spice, this is also a sadya staple.

Serves: 10

INGREDIENTS

Ripe pineapple, cut into small cubes: 2 cups

Green chillies, slit: 2

Shallots, sliced: 4

Ginger, chopped fine or julienned: 1-inch piece

Salt: ½ tsp

Curd, beaten: ½ cup

Coconut, grated: 1 cup

Mustard seeds: 1 tsp

Cumin seeds: ¼ tsp

Oil: 2 tbsp

Mustard seeds: ½ tsp

Dry red chillies, broken into two: 3

Curry leaves: 2 sprigs

METHOD

1. Cook the pineapple pieces in a little water along with green chillies, shallots, ginger and salt. Set this aside.

2. Grind coconut, mustard seeds and cumin seeds into a paste.

3. Gently add the ground paste into the cooked pineapple. Let it come to a boil so that the flavours combine. Remove from flame and set aside to cool. Slowly add the beaten curd and mix well. Transfer to a serving bowl.

4. Heat oil in a pan and splutter mustard seeds. Add dry red chillies and curry leaves. Fry lightly and pour over the cooked pineapple. Mix well.

13. Pachadi from Pickled Mango

My grandmother's kitchen always had earthen jars filled with tiny tender mangoes pickled in brine which could be used for a variety of dishes like this pachadi.

Serves: 8

INGREDIENTS

Shallots, chopped: ¼ cup

Green chillies, chopped: ½ tbsp

Ginger, chopped finely: ½ tsp

Curry leaves: 1 sprig

Mango, chopped finely: 1 cup

Brine: ¼ cup

Coconut milk extracted from 1 cup grated coconut: ½ cup

For tempering

Oil: 2 tbsp

Mustard seeds: ½ tsp

Fenugreek seeds: A pinch

Shallots, sliced: 1 tbsp

Dry red chillies, cut into 6 pcs: 3

METHOD

1. Mix and crush shallots, green chillies and ginger together. Add the chopped mango, brine and coconut milk. Mix well.

2. Heat oil in a small wok. Splutter mustard seeds, fenugreek seeds, followed by other ingredients. Fry and pour over the curry.

14. Yellow Cucumber Pachadi

Yet another staple made with curd and coconut, this goes well with hot steamed rice.

Serves: 6

INGREDIENTS

Oil: 2 tbsp

Mustard seeds: ½ tsp

Shallots, sliced: ½ cup

Ginger, minced: 1 tsp

Green chillies, minced: 1 tbsp

Curry leaves: 2 sprigs

Dry red chillies: 2

Salt to taste

Yellow cucumber, chopped into small pcs: 1 cup

Coconut, shredded: 1 cup, and ½ cup of water to extract 1½ cup of milk

Cumin seeds: ½ tsp

Mustard seeds, crushed: 1 tsp

Curd: 1 cup

METHOD

1. Heat oil in a wok. Splutter mustard seeds. Sauté shallots, ginger, green chillies, curry leaves and halved dry red chillies. Add cucumber and continue sautéing. Mix cumin and mustard seeds with the shredded coconut, blend it in a mixer and extract the coconut milk. Add the coconut milk to the cucumber mix and salt to taste. Bring this to a slight boil and switch off the flame. Allow it to cool. Beat the curd and add to the mixture. Serve.

15. Mango Pachadi

Pachadi with raw mangoes for those who like that extra tang.

Serves: 8

INGREDIENTS

Coconut oil: 2 tbsp

Raw mangoes, peeled and chopped: 1 cup

Shallots, sliced: ½ cup

Ginger, minced: 1 tbsp

Green chillies, cut in rounds: 3

Mustard seeds, crushed: 1 tbsp

Salt to taste

Coconut milk: 1 cup

Mustard seeds: 1 tsp

Shallots: 4

Dry red chillies: 2

Curry leaves: 2 sprigs

METHOD

1. Heat oil in a wok. Sauté shallots, ginger and green chillies. Add salt and mangoes, and continue sautéing. Add crushed mustard seeds and sauté again. Add coconut milk and mix well. Do not allow it to boil. Switch off the flame.

2. Heat a tablespoon of oil. Add mustard seeds and let them splutter. Add shallots, curry leaves and dry red chillies and fry lightly. Pour over the curry and serve.

16. Jackfruit Seed, Drumstick and Mango Curry

Jackfruit seeds can be used in several dishes; the combination with drumsticks and raw mangoes is delicious.

Serves: 10

INGREDIENTS

Jackfruit seeds, skin scraped off and cut lengthwise into 4 pcs: 1 cup

Drumsticks, skinned and cut into 10 pcs: 2

Mango slices: ½ cup

Shallots, sliced: ¼ cup

Turmeric powder: ¼ tsp

Cumin seeds: ¼ tsp

Grated coconut: 1 cup

Green chillies, slit: 6

Curry leaves: 2 sprigs

Salt to taste

Oil: 2 tsp

Mustard seeds: 1 tsp

Dry red chillies: 3

METHOD

1. Cook the jackfruit seeds in a pressure cooker with 2 cups boiling water for two whistles.

2. Cook drumsticks and mango slices along with shallots, 5 green chillies and curry leaves in a separate vessel.

3. Coarsely grind coconut with turmeric powder, cumin seeds and 1 green chilli.

4. Mix the jackfruit seeds, drumsticks and mango pieces together. Add the ground ingredients and mix them well. Add 1 cup water or as required to make the gravy. Add salt, and cook until done. Heat oil in a pan and splutter mustard seeds. Lightly fry dry red chillies and curry leaves. Mix and serve.

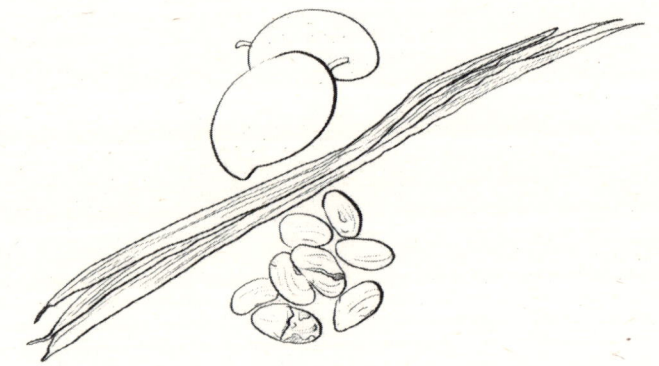

17. Theeyal

With grated coconut slow roasted to a rich dark brown colour and ground along with tamarind, chilli,
coriander and other ingredients, this sadya staple is an explosion of flavours.

Serves: 6

INGREDIENTS
Brinjal: 250 g

Coconut, grated: 2 cups

Shallots, whole: 1 tbsp

Curry leaves: 1 sprig

Green chillies, slit: 3

Coriander seeds: 1 tsp

Turmeric powder: ¼ tsp

Whole dry red chillies: 5

Tamarind: 1 gooseberry-sized
ball

Water: 1 cup

Oil: 1 tbsp

Salt: 1 tsp

For tempering
Oil: 1 tsp

Mustard seeds: 1 tsp

Curry leaves: 2 sprigs

Shallots: 3

Dry red chilli: 1

METHOD
1. Soak tamarind in 1 cup water. Strain and keep aside.

2. Cut the brinjal into inch-long pieces and then cut them lengthwise into smaller pieces. Keep them aside.

3. In a pan, heat oil and splutter mustard seeds. Add dry red chillies, curry leaves and shallots. Fry lightly and add the chopped brinjal and sauté.

4. In a heavy-bottomed pan or wok, lightly roast the grated coconut, coriander seeds, turmeric and chilli powders, dry red chillies, shallots and curry leaves. Grind the roasted ingredients into a paste without using water.

5. Add this to the brinjal mixture. Add the strained tamarind water and salt to taste. Let it simmer till the gravy turns thick.

18. Ripe Mango Curry

Small, sweet mangoes used whole work best for this curry.

Serves: 6

INGREDIENTS

Small ripe mangoes: 500 g

Green chillies, slit: 4

Chilli powder: 1 tsp

Turmeric powder: ½ tsp

Cumin powder: ½ tsp

Curry leaves: 2 sprigs

Coconut milk: ½ cup

Water: 1 cup

Salt: 1 tsp

For tempering

Oil: 1 tsp

Mustard seeds: ½ tsp

Dry red chillies: 2

Curry leaves: 2 sprigs

METHOD

1. Peel and discard the mango skin. Cook the mangoes in 1 cup water along with chilli and turmeric powders, green chillies, curry leaves and salt. When cooked, remove from flame and leave it to cool.

2. Mix cumin powder in coconut milk.

3. Add the cumin-laced coconut to the mango curry. Mix well and set aside.

4. Heat oil in a pan and splutter mustard seeds. Add dry red chillies and curry leaves and fry lightly. Pour over the curry. Serve.

19. Okra Curry

A simple dish that pairs well with both rice and chapatis.

Serves: 10

INGREDIENTS

Okra (lady's finger), cut into medium-sized pcs: 2 cups

Onions, sliced: ½ cup

Ginger, sliced: 1 tsp

Green chillies, slit: 5

Coriander powder: 1 tsp

Chilli powder: ¼ tsp

Turmeric powder: ¼ tsp

Pepper powder: ¼ tsp

Aniseed: ¼ tsp

Cinnamon: 1-inch piece

Cloves: 4

Cardamom pods: 2

Curry leaves: 2 sprigs

Lime juice: 1 tbsp

Coconut, grated: ½ cup, to extract:

Thick coconut milk: ½ cup

Thin coconut milk: 1½ cups

Oil: ¼ cup

Salt: 1 tsp

METHOD

1. Wash and dry the okra. Cut into 1-inch pieces and set aside.

2. Grind coriander, chilli, turmeric and pepper powders along with aniseed, cinnamon, cardamom and cloves into a paste. Set aside.

3. Heat oil in a pan, sauté the okra and set aside.

4. In the same pan, lightly fry onions, ginger, green chillies and curry leaves. Add the ground paste and sauté till the oil separates. Pour the thin coconut milk into the pan and bring it to a boil.

5. Then, add the sautéed okra, salt and lime juice. Simmer on low flame until the gravy becomes thick. Add the thick coconut milk. Once it begins to boil, remove from flame and serve.

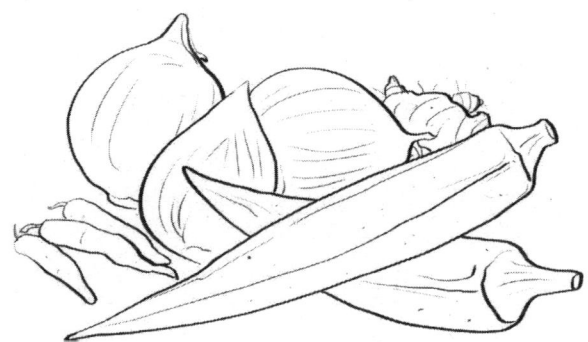

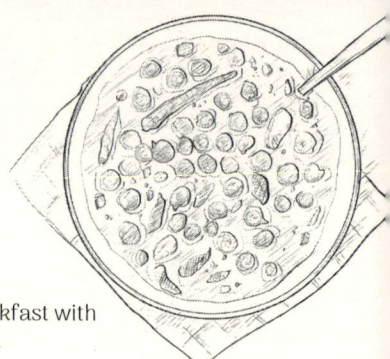

20. Masala Kadala

Kadala curry is a favourite in most Malayali homes, and is served for breakfast with puttu or pooris, with rice for lunch and with chapatis for dinner.

Serves: 20

INGREDIENTS

Black channa (black chickpea): 2 cups

Potatoes, cubed: ½ cup

Bread, cubed: ½ cup

Tomatoes, thinly sliced: 2

Onions, sliced: 1½ cups

Green chillies, slit: 6

Mustard seeds: ½ tsp

Coriander powder: 1 tbsp

Chilli powder: 1 tbsp

Turmeric powder: ¼ tsp

Mustard seeds: ½ tsp

Sugar: ½ tsp

Coriander leaves: 1 tbsp

Lime, quartered: 1

Water: 4½ cups

Oil: 1½ cups

Salt: 1 tsp

METHOD

1. Wash and soak the chickpeas overnight in 2 cups water. Pressure cook with salt in 2½ cups water for 40 minutes. Set aside.

2. In a wok, heat 1 cup oil. Fry one cup onions until golden brown, drain and set aside. Fry the bread cubes until crisp and set aside. Finally, fry the potatoes until done and set aside.

3. In the same wok, sauté green chillies and tomatoes. Remove from flame and sprinkle sugar and salt on all the fried ingredients.

4. In another pan, heat the remaining ½ cup oil. Splutter mustard seeds, and add the remaining ½ cup onions. Sauté them until brown.

5. Mix coriander, chilli and turmeric powders with a little water and make a thick paste. Reduce the flame and add this to the pan. Sauté for a few minutes and add the cooked chickpeas with the residue and mix. Remove from the flame.

6. Transfer the cooked chickpeas to a serving dish and garnish with fried onions, bread cubes, potatoes, green chillies and tomatoes. Top the curry with coriander leaves and lime quarters.

21. Kappa Purattiyathu

Soft mashed tapioca with coconut and spices is a Malayali favourite, especially with red fish curry.

Serves: 8

INGREDIENTS

Tapioca: 1 kg

Coconut, grated: 1 cup

Garlic cloves: 4

Chilli powder: ½ tsp

Turmeric powder: ¼ tsp

Cumin seeds: ¼ tsp

Salt: 1 tsp

Oil: 2 tbsp

Mustard seeds: ½ tsp

Shallots: 2 tbsp

Coconut, grated (optional): 2 tbsp

Dry red chillies, broken into two: 2

Curry leaves: 1 sprig

METHOD

1. Peel the tapioca, chop into small pieces and cook in salt water (the pieces should be fully immersed). Once cooked, drain the water and keep the tapioca aside.

2. Coarsely grind coconut, chilli and turmeric powders along with garlic and cumin seeds.

3. Make a small well in the cooked tapioca and add the ground coconut mixture and salt and leave to cook on a low flame for a few minutes. Remove, mash, mix well and keep aside.

4. Heat oil in a pan and add mustard seeds. When they splutter, add shallots, dry red chillies cut into two, grated coconut and curry leaves. Fry lightly and add this to the tapioca mix. Mix well and serve hot.

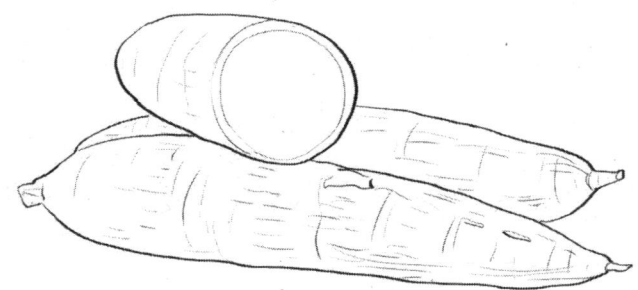

22. Mezhukkupuratti

The name may be a mouthful for a non-Malayali, but basically all it means is to sauté with shallots and spices—a simple and tasty way to prepare almost any vegetable.

Serves: 8

INGREDIENTS

Yam, cut into small pcs: 2 cups

Shallots: 2 tbsp

Garlic: 6 cloves

Dry red chillies: 3

Peppercorns: ½ tsp

Curry leaves: 2 sprigs

Water: 4 cups

Oil: 2 tbsp

Salt: ½ tsp

METHOD

1. Coarsely crush garlic, shallots, dry red chillies and peppercorns. Keep aside.

2. Wash the yam pieces twice and cook them in water and salt. After it is cooked, drain out the excess water. Keep aside.

3. In a wok, heat oil. Add crushed ingredients and sauté well. Add curry leaves and the cooked yam. Stir fry on a low flame till the yam pieces are coated with the garlic and shallot mixture. Remove from the flame and serve hot.

Note: Yam can be substituted with green plantain or beans.

Sambar

Mango Rasam

Avial

Erissery

Pachadis

Jackfruit Seed, Drumstick and Mango Curry

Theeyal

Ripe Mango Curry

Masala Kadala

Kappa Purattiyathu

Mezhukkupuratti

Assorted Vegetable Chips

Dal Kurma

Assorted Vegetarian Dishes

Lime Rice

Mutton Biryani

All Flavour Pudding with Chocolate Sauce

Assorted Payasams

Thai Pudding

Tender Coconut Soufflé

Egg Curd Soup

Bharani Soup

Tomato Soup

Assorted Pickles

Assorted Pickles and Chutney Powders

Mangoes in Brine

Chutney for Boiled Tapioca

23. Okra Fry

Quick and easy to make, this is a good side dish for weekday lunches.

Serves: 6

INGREDIENTS

Okra: 250 g

Gram flour: 2 tbsp

Chilli powder: 1 tsp

Asafoetida: ½ tsp

Oil: 1 cup

Salt: ½ tsp

METHOD

1. Wash and dry the okra well. Slice them into thin pieces lengthwise.

2. Marinate the okra in a mixture of chilli powder, asafoetida and salt for about 5 minutes.

3. In a heavy-bottomed pan, heat the oil. Sprinkle okra with gram flour and toss. Deep fry in hot oil. Serve hot.

24. Kaya Varuthathu

These banana chips can be sliced round, halved, quartered, wafer-thin or chunky. Plain or spiced, whichever way you make them, they are delicious.

Yields: 200 g

INGREDIENTS

Banana: ½ kg

Oil: 2—3 cups

Water: 2 cups

Salt: 2 tsp

METHOD

1. Skin the bananas. Wash and dry them.

2. Slice them into thin round slices, the thinner the better. Make sure they are of the same thickness so that they get fried uniformly.

3. Heat water and dissolve salt in it. Keep this aside.

4. Heat oil in a heavy-bottomed wok and deep fry the sliced bananas in small batches till golden brown. Carefully add 2 tbsp of the salt water into the oil.

5. The oil will splutter and froth up. Let the fried bananas absorb the salt. Once the oil has stopped spluttering and frothing, use a slotted spoon and remove the fried banana chips. Place them in a strainer to drain out excess oil.

6. Repeat this till all the banana chips have been fried.

7. When cool, store in an airtight container to keep the chips crisp.

25. Fried Bitter Gourd

A great way to enjoy bitter gourd; it can also be dried and stored to fry when required.

Serves: 8

INGREDIENTS

Bitter gourd: 500 g

Coconut, thinly sliced (optional): ½ cup

Onion, finely sliced: ½ cup

Green chillies, slit: 6

Chilli powder: 1 tsp

Oil: ½ cup

Salt: ½ tsp

METHOD

1. Wash the bitter gourd, pat dry, slit it open and discard the seeds. Slice it into thin round discs.

2. Mix bitter gourd slices with coconut bits, green chillies, chilli powder and salt. Marinate for 10 minutes. Squeeze out the excess water.

3. In a heavy-bottomed pan, heat oil and fry onions until golden brown. Drain and keep aside.

4. Fry the bitter gourd slices with coconut bits and green chillies. When crisp, remove from the oil with a slotted spoon and drain out the oil.

5. Mix the fried onions with fried bitter gourd and serve.

26. Kachiya Moru

A Malayali's lunch isn't complete without kachiya moru.

Serves: 12

INGREDIENTS

Curd: 6 cups

Coconut, grated: 1 cup

Shallots: 3

Garlic cloves, sliced: 2

Ginger, julienned: 1-inch piece

Green chillies: 3

Turmeric powder: ¼ tsp

Cumin seeds: ¼ tsp

Curry leaves: 1 sprig

Salt: 1 tsp

Oil: 1 tsp

Mustard seeds: ½ tsp

Fenugreek seeds: ¼ tsp

Dry red chillies: 2

Chilli powder: A pinch

METHOD

1. In a heavy-bottomed pan, mix beaten curd, turmeric powder, ginger, curry leaves and salt.

2. Grind coconut, shallots, garlic cloves, green chillies and cumin seeds together to a fine paste. Add a little beaten curd to the paste and mix well. Then add the rest of the curd into it. Transfer the mix to the pan.

3. Keep on a low flame and stir continuously. As soon as the steam appears, remove from the flame. Keep stirring until it cools.

4. Heat oil in a pan. Splutter mustard seeds, add fenugreek seeds and dry red chillies. Add a pinch of red chilli powder. Fry lightly, and cool before adding into the curry.

27. Spinach (Cheera) Cutlet

A great way to use spinach; these cutlets make great starters too.

Yields: 8

INGREDIENTS

Oil: 4 tsp

Onion, chopped: ¼ cup

Green chilli, sliced: 1 tsp

Spinach, chopped: 2 cups

Potato, boiled and mashed: ½ cup

Salt to taste

For the filling

Coconut, grated: ½ cup

Green chilli, whole: 1

Shallots: 2

Ginger: A small piece

Salt and lemon juice to taste

Sugar: A pinch

Gram flour: ½ cup

Breadcrumbs: 1½ cups

Oil to deep fry

METHOD

1. Heat oil in a pan and sauté onions and green chillies.

2. Add spinach, mix well and cook covered. Sprinkle a little water if needed. When the spinach is done, add mashed potatoes and salt. Mix this well and make lemon-sized balls when cool enough to handle.

To make the filling

1. Coarsely grind grated coconut, green chilli, shallots, ginger, lemon juice, sugar and salt to taste.

2. Take a spinach-potato ball, flatten slightly and place a spoonful of the filling in the centre. Bring the edges together to form the cutlet in a triangle shape. Dip this in a medium loose batter made of gram flour and water. Add a pinch of salt in the batter. Coat with breadcrumbs and deep fry in oil.

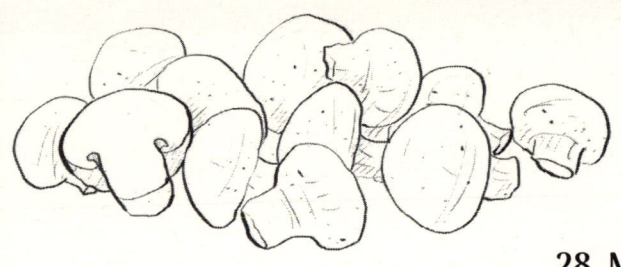

28. Mushroom Packets

Mushrooms in a crepe are given a Kerala touch by the addition of green chillies and pepper.

Yields: 12

INGREDIENTS

Refined flour: 1 cup

Egg, beaten: 1

Milk: 1 cup

Water: 1 cup

Salt to taste

For the filling

Oil: 2 tbsp

Onion, chopped: 1 large

Green chilli, chopped: 1

Ginger, chopped: 1 tsp

Green capsicum, chopped: ½

Pepper powder: ½ tsp

Celery stalks, chopped: 2

Button mushrooms, sliced: 250 g

Salt to taste

For the white sauce

Butter: 1 heaped tsp

Refined flour: 1 tsp

Milk: ¼ cup

Grated cheese to taste

Egg, beaten: 1

Breadcrumbs for coating

METHOD

1. Mix the beaten egg with flour. Add milk slowly so that lumps don't form. Add water, salt to taste and mix well to make a loose batter.

2. Rest the batter for 30 minutes.

3. Heat a saucepan. Grease the surface lightly. Do not overheat the pan. Pour a small ladleful of the batter and give it a swirl so that it spreads evenly and thinly. As soon as it is done, turn it over on a clean, flat surface. Continue making pancakes with the rest of the batter.

To make the filling

1. Heat some oil in a wok. Sauté onions, green chillies and ginger. Keep stirring until the onions are transparent. Add capsicum, pepper powder, celery and mushrooms. Keep stirring till the water from the mushrooms is absorbed. Remove from heat and set aside.

To make the white sauce

1. Heat a pan and melt butter. Add flour and keep stirring till it thickens. Slowly add milk and stir till a smooth, thick sauce is formed. Add grated cheese, mix well.

2. Pour this sauce into the sautéed mushrooms.

3. Take a pancake, place a spoonful of the mixture in the middle and bring one half of the pancake to the centre. Let the other half overlap. Seal the edges with water. Dip each packet into the beaten egg and coat with breadcrumbs. Fry in hot oil and serve.

Note: As an alternative, cut the packet into half, diagonally and serve.

29. Dal Kurma

A great side dish for chapatis, this combination of dal and vegetables in a rich creamy gravy makes it a full meal.

Serves: 15

INGREDIENTS

Carrot, beans, cabbage, chopped fine: 2 cups

Split green gram: 1 cup

Ghee: 1 tbsp

Onions, sliced thin: ½ cup

Turmeric powder: 1 tsp

Cloves: 9

Cardamom: 6

Cinnamon stick: 6 pcs

Garlic paste: 2 tsp

Ginger paste: 2 tsp

Coriander powder: 2 tsp

Chilli powder: 1 tsp

Coconut milk: 1 cup

Coconut, grated: ½ cup

Curd: ¼ cup

Cashew nuts, ground: 1 tbsp

Salt to taste

Green chillies, slit: 6

Ripe tomatoes: 2

Lime juice: 1 tbsp

Coriander leaves: ½ cup

METHOD

1. Steam the vegetables till they are half-cooked. Make a paste of chilli, turmeric and coriander powders. Set this aside.

2. Pressure cook the split green gram for 2 whistles till a half cup of residue remains. Sauté onions in ghee and oil. Add garlic, sauté again. Then add the spices, ginger and garlic pastes, followed by the coriander and chilli paste (given in Step 1). Sauté well. Add tomatoes and stir again. Add the cooked green gram along with the gravy. Add coconut milk, salt to taste and stir well. If more gravy is required, add thin coconut milk. Grind cashew nuts to a paste, mix with curd and add to the gravy. Allow this to simmer and add the vegetables. Add slit green chillies, lime juice and coriander leaves. Mix well and remove from the flame.

Rice Dishes

1. Mutton Biryani
2. Prawn Biryani
3. Special Ghee Rice
4. Coconut Rice

5. Lime Rice
6. Tomato Coconut Rice
7. Mushroom Biryani

1. Mutton Biryani

Biryani is made in different ways all over India. In this recipe, meat and rice are cooked separately and then layered and baked.

Serves: 8

INGREDIENTS

Mutton kurma: See recipe on page 57

Basmati rice: 3 cups

Cloves: 8

Cinnamon: 4-inch piece

Cardamoms, crushed: 8

Bay leaves: 4

Coriander leaves: 2 cups

Mint leaves: 2 cups

Juice of a lime

Onion, finely sliced: 1 cup

Raisins: ¼ cup

Cashew nuts: ¼ cup

Water: 6 cups

Salt to taste

Ghee: ½ cup

Piece of damp cloth

METHOD

1. Preheat the oven to 350°F.

2. Prepare the mutton kurma and keep it aside.

3. Soak rice in water for 15 minutes. Wash it well and drain the water through a strainer.

4. Boil 6 cups water with salt, cinnamon, cloves, cardamoms, bay leaves, coriander and mint leaves. Cook the rice in this. Add the juice of 1 lime. Stir well. Once the rice is cooked, drain the water and keep it aside.

5. In a pan or wok, heat ghee and fry onions until they are golden brown. Then, remove from the pan.

6. Fry cashew nuts and raisins separately. Drain and keep them aside.

7. Grease a wide, heavy-bottomed vessel with ghee. Arrange a small amount of rice on the bottom layer of the vessel and scatter a tablespoon of fried onions on it. Arrange the mutton pieces. Follow this with another layer of rice, and continue layering with the gravy and mutton pieces. Add chopped mint and coriander leaves. Finally, top with a layer of rice. Drizzle some ghee on the topmost rice layer. Cover with a damp cloth. Place a lid on top and leave this to bake (350°F) for 30 minutes.

8. While serving, garnish with fried onions, cashew nuts and raisins. Make sure not to mix the biryani. It should be served by scooping from the bottom layer, starting from the side of the vessel.

2. Prawn Biryani

This is a regional favourite.

Serves: 3

INGREDIENTS

Biryani rice (washed and soaked for 30 min): 1 cup

Prawns: ¼ kg

Oil: 1 tbsp

Ghee: 2 heaped tsp

Bay leaf: 1

Aniseed: ½ tsp

Onion, sliced: 1

Green chillies, slit: 2

Ginger and garlic paste: 2 heaped tsp each

Tomato, sliced: 1 large

Coriander leaves: A handful

Mint leaves: A handful

Curd: 2 tbsp

Turmeric powder: ½ tsp

Coriander powder: 1 heaped tsp

Chilli powder: ½ tsp

Garam masala: 1 tsp

Salt to taste

Coconut milk (dilute with water to make 1½ cups): ½ cup

METHOD

1. Heat oil and ghee in a pressure cooker pan. Add bay leaf and aniseed and fry. Add onions and green chillies. Sauté till they are brownish-pink in colour. Add ginger and garlic pastes and fry lightly. Add tomato followed by coriander and mint leaves. Mix in curd. Add coriander, turmeric, chilli powders and garam masala, then add the prawns. Stir for 2 minutes. Add salt and the diluted coconut milk. Let this boil, then add the washed rice. Cover the pressure cooker and let the steam escape. Place the weight and keep it on a low flame. Cook for 10 minutes.

Note: If you are not using a pressure cooker, add an extra ½ cup water, and let it cook with a closed lid.

3. Special Ghee Rice

Malayalis love ghee rice and it is made both with Basmati as well as the short-grained jeera rice.

Serves: 6

INGREDIENTS

Biryani or jeera rice: 3 cups

Cloves: 6

Cinnamon: 2-inch pcs
(a couple)

Cardamoms: 6

Coconut milk from 1 coconut:
6 cups

Ghee: 3 tbsp

For the ground paste

Dry red chillies: 4

Coriander powder: 1 tsp

Ginger-garlic paste: 1 tsp

Shallots: 10

Cumin seeds: 1 tsp

Cloves: 4

Cinnamon: 1-inch piece

Oil: ¼ cup

Juice from half a lime

Onions, big, sliced: 2

Saffron: ½ tsp dissolved in
1 tbsp milk

Salt to taste

METHOD

1. Preheat the oven to 350°F.

2. Grind dry red chillies, coriander powder, ginger-garlic paste, shallots, cumin seeds, cloves and cinnamon into a fine paste.

3. Mix with coconut milk, strain and keep aside.

4. Heat a pan and sauté cloves, cinnamon and cardamoms in ghee.

5. Add rice and fry until light brown. Add coconut milk and salt to taste. Cook till done.

6. Heat a pan and fry the sliced onions in oil, and when done, keep this aside.

7. Grease the bottom of a vessel with ghee.

8. Transfer the rice to this vessel, drizzle lime juice and strained saffron.

9. Cover the rice with a wet cloth. Bake in a 350°F oven for 30 minutes.

10. Garnish with fried onions. Serve hot.

4. Coconut Rice

Rice is cooked in coconut milk and then garnished with roasted coconut.

Serves: 4

INGREDIENTS

Basmati rice: 2 cups

Coconut, grated: ¼ cup

Coconut milk: 5 cups

Ghee: ¼ cup

Salt: 1 tsp

METHOD

1. Soak rice in water for 15 minutes. Wash it well and drain out the water.

2. In a heavy-bottomed pan, heat ghee. Fry the washed rice in it till it turns light brown in colour.

3. Then add coconut milk and bring it to a boil. Add salt, and leave to simmer on a low flame till the coconut milk is absorbed and the rice is well-cooked.

4. In a separate pan, lightly roast grated coconut for garnishing.

5. Transfer the cooked rice to a serving dish and garnish with the roasted coconut. Serve hot.

5. Lime Rice

This south Indian favourite can be made with day-old rice. It remains fresh as the lime juice acts as a preservative.

Serves: 4

INGREDIENTS

Rice: 2 cups

Green chillies, chopped: ½ tsp

Turmeric powder: ½ tsp

Mustard seeds: ½ tsp

Bengal gram: 2 tbsp

Dry red chillies: 3

Sugar: ½ tsp

Lime juice: 2 tbsp

Ghee: 2 tbsp

Oil: 3 tbsp

Salt to taste

Garnish

Onion, finely sliced: ½ cup

Potatoes, sliced: ½ cup

Raisins: 1 tbsp

Coriander leaves: ¼ cup

Oil: ¾ cup

METHOD

1. Cook the rice. When it is done, add ghee, sugar, lime juice and salt. Mix well and set aside.

2. In a heavy-bottomed pan or wok, heat oil. Splutter mustard seeds, add Bengal gram, dry red chillies, turmeric powder and green chillies. Fry lightly and then mix into the rice.

3. Heat oil and fry the potatoes, onions and raisins separately. Remove and set aside.

4. Transfer the cooked rice to a serving dish and garnish with potatoes, onions and raisins. Sprinkle coriander leaves before serving.

6. Tomato Coconut Rice

Combining the tartness of tomatoes with the creaminess of coconut,
this can make a complete meal with just pickles and papadams.

Serves: 4

INGREDIENTS

Basmati rice: ½ kg (2 cups)

Tomatoes: 1½ cups

Thick coconut milk from 1½ coconuts: 3 cups

Butter, melted: 2 tbsp

Onions, small size, chopped: 2

Cinnamon: 2 1-inch pcs

Cloves: 5

Cardamoms: 5

Green chillies: 1 tsp

Garlic paste: 1 tsp

Coriander leaves, chopped: A small bunch

Salt to taste

METHOD

1. Soak rice in water for 15 minutes. Wash and drain it.

2. Extract 2 cups of tomato puree in a blender after blanching the tomatoes. Mix the puree and coconut milk together. Set aside.

3. Heat a pan and melt butter. Add all the spices and sauté for 30 seconds. Add onions, green chillies and garlic paste. Sauté until the onions are soft. Add the rice and fry well. Pour the coconut milk and tomato puree mixture, add salt to taste. Cover with a lid and cook on a medium flame. Once cooked, remove from the flame.

4. While serving, garnish with chopped coriander leaves.

7. Mushroom Biryani

A great option for vegetarians.

Serves: 3

INGREDIENTS

Rice, washed and soaked for 30 minutes: 1 cup

Coconut milk: ½ cup (dilute with 1½ cups water)

Mushrooms, washed and quartered: 1 packet

Ghee: 2 heaped tsp

Oil: 1 tbsp

Bay leaf: 1

Aniseed: ½ tsp

Onion, sliced: 1

Green chillies, slit: 2

Ginger and garlic paste: 1 tsp each

Tomato, chopped into small pcs: 1

Handful of mint and coriander leaves

Curd: ½ cup

Turmeric powder: ½ tsp

Coriander powder: 1 heaped tsp

Chilli powder: ½ tsp

Garam masala: 1 tsp

Salt to taste

METHOD

1. Heat oil and ghee. Add bay leaf and aniseed. Fry for a couple of minutes. Add onions and green chillies and keep stirring until the onions turn light brown. At this point, add ginger and garlic paste. Sauté well. Add chopped tomato and stir. Mix in curd. Add the turmeric, coriander and chilli powders and garam masala. Fry lightly. Add mushrooms, stir for 2 minutes. Add salt to taste. Pour the diluted coconut milk. Allow it to boil and then add the washed rice. Transfer this to a pressure cooker. Cover with a lid and allow the steam to escape. Place a weight on the cooker and reduce the flame. Leave it to cook for 5 minutes. This can be cooked in a pan by adding ½ cup extra water.

2. Add chopped coriander and mint leaves. Serve hot with sweet pickle and papadams.

Payasam and Puddings

1. Pal Payasam

Made with just a few ingredients, this tastes like the famous Ambalapuzha Pal Payasam.

Serves: 8

INGREDIENTS

Broken raw rice: ½ cup

Water: 2 cups

Milk: 2 l

Condensed milk: 1 tin

Sugar: ¼ cup

Cardamom powder: 1 tsp

Cashew nuts, slivered: ½ cup

METHOD

1. Wash and cook the rice in 2 cups water. Then add milk. Cook the rice till the milk is reduced to 1 cup. Add condensed milk and sugar, stir well. Add cashew nuts. Take a little milk and mix cardamom powder without forming any lumps. Strain this into the payasam.

2. Sprinkle cashew nuts and remove from the flame.

2. Parippu Payasam

Special to Kerala, this dessert made with split green gram, coconut milk, jaggery and ghee, is rich and delicious.

Serves: 15

INGREDIENTS

Coconuts, grated: 4

Split green gram: 3 cups

Water: 4 cups

Sago: ½ cup

Water: 8 cups

Ghee: ½ cup

Coconut slivers: 2 tbsp

Cashew nuts: 2 heaped tbsp

Raisins: 2 tbsp

Jaggery: 1 kg

Water: 10 cups

Dried ginger powder: ½ tsp

Cardamom powder: 1 tsp

Cumin powder: ½ tsp

METHOD

1. Extract 3 cups of thick milk from the grated coconut and keep aside. Add water and extract another 6 cups of thin milk.

2. Roast the green gram in a heavy skillet over a low to medium flame till they release a nutty aroma.

3. Wash and cook the gram in 8 cups water till they are soft and the water has been absorbed.

4. Boil 4 cups water. Add sago and cook till it is transparent. Drain off the water and wash in cold water. Strain and keep aside.

5. Fry coconut slivers, cashew nuts and raisins in 2 tbsp ghee. Keep this aside.

6. Mix 10 cups water with jaggery and melt over a low heat. Strain the jaggery syrup into the cooked gram and continue cooking. In between, stir in the remaining ghee. Simmer gently, and as it thickens, add 6 cups of the thin coconut milk. To this, add powdered spices mixed in the 1st extract of coconut milk (3 cups), and sago. Mix well. Do not allow this to boil. Finally, garnish with coconut slivers, cashew nuts and raisins. Stir well and remove from the flame.

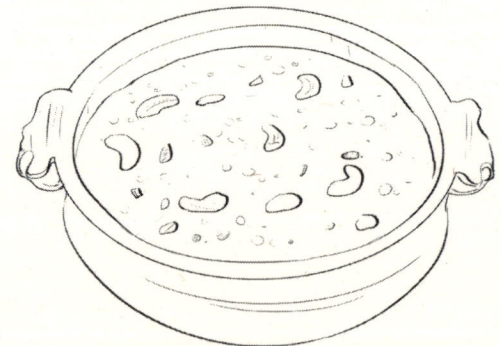

3. Pressure Cooker Payasam

When in a hurry, turn to the trusty pressure cooker and you have this delicious dessert in a jiffy.

Serves: 8

INGREDIENTS

Milk: 1 l

Basmati rice: 1 tbsp

Sugar: 4 tbsp

Cardamom pods: 4

Cashew nut or almond slivers: ¼ cup

METHOD

1. Boil milk in a pressure cooker pan without the lid. Wash the rice and add it to the boiled milk. Add all the other ingredients except nuts and pressure cook.

2. At the first whistle, reduce the flame. Leave it to simmer for 30 minutes. Turn off the flame, open the cooker and mix the cashew nut or almond slivers. Cover and cook again for 15 minutes. Let the flavours settle.

3. Remove the cardamom pods before serving.

4. Tender Coconut Soufflé

This is one of my personal favourites, with bite-sized tender coconut pieces.

Serves: 10

INGREDIENTS

Condensed milk: 1 tin

Milk: 2 tins

Sugar: 8 tbsp

China grass: 10 g

Water: 1½ cups

Tender coconut water: 1 tin

Slivers of tender coconut:
½ cup

Coconut, finely grated: ¼ cup

Sugar: 1 tbsp

METHOD

1. In a heavy-bottomed pan, warm milk, sugar and condensed milk. Keep stirring till the sugar is dissolved. Keep this aside.

2. Cut the China grass into small bits and rinse in water. Place the pieces in a strainer and allow the water to drain. Then, dissolve the pieces in 1½ cups water. Keep it on a low flame and stir constantly till the pieces dissolve completely. Take off the flame and add tender coconut water. Strain into the condensed milk mixture. Mix well.

3. Pour into a glass pudding dish or individual ramekin bowls.

4. Scatter the slivers of tender coconut on top of the pudding. Set in the refrigerator.

For the topping

1. Heat a small wok and dry roast the finely grated coconut with sugar. Keep stirring, and when it turns brown, remove from the flame and store in airtight bottles.

2. Sprinkle this on top of the pudding before serving.

5. Thai Pudding with Jaggery Syrup

Sago forms the body of this pudding, flavoured with jaggery, coconut milk and rose essence.

Serves: 10

INGREDIENTS

Sago: 2 cups

Water: 8 cups

Gelatine: 1 tsp

Water: 2 tbsp

Sugar: 6 tsp

Rose essence: 1 drop

For the syrup

Jaggery: 250 g

Water: 1½ cups

Coconut, grated: 2 cups

Thick coconut milk: 1 cup

METHOD

1. Boil sago in water. Drain and wash thoroughly in cold water to remove all the starch. Keep it aside.

2. Soak gelatine in cold water and dissolve by double boiling.

3. Add the melted gelatine, sugar and rose essence to the prepared sago.

4. Pour this into a mould and set in the refrigerator.

5. Crush jaggery into small pieces. Add water and cook to reduce the jaggery syrup to 1 cup. Strain the syrup to remove the sediments.

6. Extract 1 cup thick coconut milk from 2 cups of grated coconut.

7. To serve, unmould the sago pudding into a bowl and pour ¼ cup of coconut milk over it. Drizzle 2 tbsp of jaggery syrup on top. Serve the pudding with the remaining coconut milk and jaggery syrup.

6. Chocolate Tart

A crunchy tart base and chocolatey filling make this a perennial favourite.

Serves: 6

INGREDIENTS

For the base

Flour: 200 g

Icing sugar: 1 tbsp

Chilled butter: 100 g

Ice water: A little

For the filling

Cooking chocolate: 70 g

Eggs: 2

Butter: 100 g

Condensed milk: 1 tin

Walnuts, chopped: 100 g (optional)

Vanilla essence: 1 tsp

METHOD

1. Preheat the oven to 350°F.

2. Grease an 8-inch tart pan with butter and line with butter paper.

3. Sieve flour and icing sugar. Rub the butter into the flour with your fingertips. Add a little ice water to make a rough dough. Keep this covered with a damp cloth in the fridge.

4. Roll out the dough and place it in the tart pan. Prick the surface with a fork and half-bake the tart in the oven.

METHOD

For the filling

1. Beat the eggs, add the condensed milk and continue beating till it is frothy. Keep aside. Melt chocolate and butter in a double boiler. Add vanilla essence, walnuts and the egg mix. Pour this mixture into the half-baked tart base. Bake for 20 minutes or till done.

7. Chocolate Soufflé

This recipe tells you how to get that soufflé light as air.

Serves: 10

INGREDIENTS

Gelatine: 2 tsp

Water: 3 tbsp

Eggs: 4

Sugar: ¾ cup

Salt: 2 pinches

Milk: 2 cups

Cocoa: 2 heaped tbsp

Flour: 1 tsp

Vanilla essence: 1 tsp

Cream: ½ cup (for decoration)

Slivered almonds or cashew nuts: ½ cup

METHOD

1. In a small pan, mix gelatine in 3 tbsp cold water and keep aside.

2. Sieve cocoa and flour and mix them in ½ cup milk.

3. In a bowl, beat the egg yolks well with half the quantity of sugar and 2 pinches of salt.

4. Slowly add the rest of the milk.

5. Pour this into a pan and heat gently to make custard. Add the cocoa mixture to the custard and cook till the custard turns thick. Remove from flame and leave to cool.

6. Dissolve the gelatine mixture in a double boiler. Pour the dissolved gelatine in a steady stream into the custard. Add vanilla essence. Stir well and strain.

7. Pour the custard into a glass bowl and leave to half-set in a refrigerator.

8. Beat the egg whites stiff with the remaining sugar and vanilla essence.

9. Gently fold the beaten egg whites into the half-set custard. Pour into individual bowls or a large glass bowl. Leave in the refrigerator to set. Before serving, decorate with cream or serve with slivered nuts.

8. Festival Ice Cream

We still remember the taste of home-made ice cream and this recipe is one for keeps.

Serves: 10

INGREDIENTS

Gelatine powder: 2 tsp

Water: 2 tsp

Egg yolks: 3

Sugar: 4 tbsp

Milk: 2 cups

Condensed milk: 1 tin

Cold milk: 1 cup

Cornflour: 1½ tbsp

Vanilla essence: 1 tsp

Egg whites: 3

Sugar: 3½ tbsp

Lime juice: 1 tsp

Vanilla essence: ½ tsp

METHOD

1. In a pan, soak gelatine powder in water and keep aside. Beat the egg yolks and sugar well. Add boiled milk and then the condensed milk, beating well with each addition. Transfer to a heavy-bottomed pan. Place on a low flame and keep stirring to prevent lumps from forming. Dissolve cornflour in cold milk and pour into the custard. Continue stirring till the custard turns thick and starts coating the back of the spoon.

2. Warm up the dissolved gelatine in 2 tbsp water and pour into the custard in a steady stream. Beat well. Remove from the fire and add vanilla essence.

3. Mix well and once cold, pour into an ice cream tray. Leave to set in the freezer overnight or for 8 hours.

4. Allow the ice cream to thaw slightly. Transfer into a mixer bowl. Beat till it froths up. Meanwhile, beat the egg whites stiff adding sugar, lime juice and vanilla essence.

5. Gently fold the egg whites into the beaten custard and leave the ice cream to set in the freezer overnight or for at least 8 hours.

9. All Flavour Pudding with Chocolate Sauce

There is a riot of flavours in this pudding, and they all go well together, from the plum
cake to the pineapple jam and the brandy, finished off with chocolate sauce.

Serves: 12

INGREDIENTS

Eggs, medium-sized: 4

Lukewarm milk: 2 cups

Condensed milk: ½ tin

Sugar: 8 tsp

Bread pcs, without the
edges, soaked in water, then
squeezed and crumbled:
½ cup

Plum cake, crumbled: ½ cup

Coconut, finely grated: 4 tsp

Pineapple jam: ¼ cup

Brandy: ½ cup

Vanilla essence: 1 tsp

For the chocolate sauce

Cocoa powder: 4 tsp

Cornflour: 2 tsp

Salt: A pinch

Cold milk: 1 cup

Milk: 1 cup

Sugar: 8 tsp

Butter: 1 tsp

METHOD

1. Whisk the eggs till light and fluffy. Pour in milk and whisk again. Add all the ingredients one by one and mix well without forming any lumps. Pour this mixture into a greased mould and cover with a lid or foil.

2. Steam in a pressure cooker by placing the mould in a shallow vessel immersed in water. Cook for 20 minutes and remove. Make sure the pressure cooker is free of steam before opening the lid. When the pudding is set, keep aside to cool. Unmould on to a glass plate. Serve with chocolate sauce.

METHOD

1. Mix cocoa, cornflour and salt in 1 cup cold milk.

2. Add sugar to the remaining milk and boil. When it boils, add the cocoa mixture very slowly and simmer the custard.

3. When thick, remove from the flame. Beat with a fork to remove any lumps, and add butter.

4. When cold, pour over the pudding. Garnish with cream, cherries and sliced bananas.

10. Julian Rock Pudding

A fruity pudding with an interesting topping.

Serves: 10

INGREDIENTS

Pineapple: 1 big tin (850 g)

Condensed milk: 1 tin

Cherries: ½ tin

Pitted apricots, stewed: 24

Brandy: 1 tbsp

For the garnish

White sesame seeds: 1 tsp

Cashew nuts, chopped: 2 tsp

Coconut, grated: 2 tbsp

Mustard seeds: ½ tsp

Sugar: 1 tbsp

Fresh cream as required

METHOD

1. Cut the pineapple into 1-inch pieces and leave it in the syrup. Add cherries without the syrup. Mix the pineapple pieces, condensed milk, cherries, stewed apricots and brandy in a bowl. Leave in the refrigerator to cool.

METHOD

1. Heat a skillet and carefully roast sesame seeds, cashew nuts, grated coconut and mustard seeds. When it turns brown, sprinkle sugar and stir continuously. When the mixture turns crisp, remove from the flame. Bottle when cool and use later as topping for the pudding.

2. To serve the pudding, pour the cooled condensed milk with the pineapple, cherry and apricot mixture into a wide glass bowl. Place blobs of cream randomly on top of the pudding. Sprinkle the prepared crispy topping.

Soups

1. Egg Curd Soup

This soup has steamed eggs in a delicious meat broth.

Serves: 6

INGREDIENTS

Eggs: 3

Milk: 2 cups

Flour: 2 tbsp

Cold milk

Salt: 2 pinches

Mutton or chicken: 250 g

Ginger, finely chopped: 2 tsp

Water: 4 cups

Vinegar: 1 tsp

Salt to taste

Butter: 1 tbsp

Cornflour: 2 tbsp

Celery, finely chopped: 1 tbsp

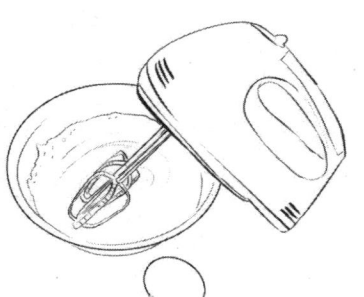

METHOD

1. Beat the eggs lightly. Add hot milk slowly, beating constantly so that the eggs don't curdle. Mix flour in cold milk and sieve it. Add this into the beaten egg milk and mix. Add salt to taste.

2. Pour this into a greased tray or vessel.

3. Steam for 30 minutes. Make sure you place a heavy object on the lid of the vessel. Remove from flame. Once the custard is set and chilled, cut into small cubes. Set aside.

4. Pressure cook mutton or chicken with ginger, vinegar, water and salt for 3 whistles. Cut the cooked meat into cubes. Set aside. Strain the remaining stock and mix in 2 cups hot water.

5. Heat butter in a pan and add cornflour and sauté until light brown. Add the stock, cubed meat and celery.

6. Double boil the soup to keep it warm. When the soup begins to bubble up, add the egg cubes gently.

7. Serve as soon as it is prepared.

Note: This soup tastes best when hot. Always double boil the soup and reheat before serving.

2. Bharani Soup

The broth is made by double boiling and uses a variety of spices.

Serves: 8

INGREDIENTS

Chicken: 500 g

Liver: 50 g

Shallots, sliced: ¼ cup

Ginger, julienned: 1 tsp

Garlic cloves: 9

Cinnamon, 1-inch pcs: 2

Cloves: 6

Cardamom pod: 1

Crushed pepper: 1 tsp

Water: 3 cups

Salt to taste

White pepper powder: 1 tsp

METHOD

1. Take a porcelain jar with a lid.

2. Chop chicken and liver into small pieces along with the bones crushed. Put this into the jar. Add shallots, ginger, garlic, cinnamon, cloves, cardamom and crushed pepper. Pour 1½ l water and mix well. Close the lid tightly.

3. Keep the jar on a shallow pan inside the pressure cooker and cover it. The cooker should have water level reaching half the height of the jar. After the first whistle, reduce the flame and let it simmer for 4 hours.

4. Strain the soup. Add salt to taste.

5. Sprinkle white pepper powder and serve hot.

3. Fish Soup

Light and nourishing, this soup is for all seasons.

Serves: 6

INGREDIENTS

Fresh fish, cleaned and sliced: 250 g

Water: 4 cups

Onions, finely chopped: ½ cup

Ginger, finely chopped: 2 tsp

Celery, finely chopped: 1 tbsp

Crushed pepper: 1 tsp

Oil: 1 tbsp

Arrowroot flour: 2 tsp

Milk: ½ cup

METHOD

1. Cook the fish in a pressure cooker along with water, onions, ginger, celery, pepper and salt. Cook for 2 whistles. Strain the stock.

2. Heat oil and roast the arrowroot flour. Add milk and keep stirring to avoid curdling and formation of lumps. Strain, add the stock and mix well. Bring to a boil and remove.

3. Add salt and pepper to taste. Serve hot.

Note: A couple of pieces of the cooked fish can be shredded and added to the soup with minced celery. If celery is not available, coriander leaves or mint leaves can be used to enhance the flavour.

This soup is light and nourishing for convalescents.

4. Vegetable Soup

Split green gram gives this soup body and richness.

Serves: 8

INGREDIENTS

Split green gram: 1 tbsp

Potato medium-sized, skinned
and chopped: 1

Onion medium-sized: 1 cut
into chunks

Ginger: ¼-inch piece

Garlic cloves: 4

Turmeric powder: ½ tsp

Peppercorns: 10

Water: 2 cups

Salt to taste

Butter: 1½ tbsp

Zucchini, cut into small bits:
½ cup

Broccoli, cut into small bits:
½ cup

Baby corn, cut into small bits:
½ cup

Sliced onions: ¼ cup

Oil: 2 tbsp

METHOD

1. Pressure cook on a medium flame the first 9 ingredients and cook for 3 whistles.

2. Transfer the cooked ingredients to a blender. Make a puree and strain it. Mix well and set aside.

3. Melt butter in a pan. Sauté zucchini, broccoli and baby corn. Add the sautéed vegetables to the soup. Mix well.

4. Heat oil in a pan and fry onions sliced thinly. Top the soup with fried onions and serve.

5. Tomato Soup

A favourite with young and old alike.

Serves: 6

INGREDIENTS

Ripe tomatoes: 1½ cups

Onions: ½ cup

Carrots: ½ cup

Water: 3 cups

Butter: 1 tbsp

Arrowroot flour: 1 tbsp

Tomato sauce: ½ cup

Sugar to taste

Salt: As required

METHOD

1. Pressure cook tomatoes, carrots and onions with water. Cook for 2 whistles. Blend the ingredients and strain the soup.

2. Heat a heavy-bottomed pan, melt butter and add the flour. Sauté on a low flame until light brown and add the soup. Blend well until smooth.

3. Finally, mix in the tomato sauce. Add sugar and salt to taste.

6. Drumsticks and Bottle Gourd Soup

This unusual soup is very nutritious.

Serves: 4

INGREDIENTS

Drumsticks: 4

Bottle gourd: ½

Water: 3 cups

Olive oil: 1 tsp

Ginger, chopped: 1-inch piece

Salt to taste

Pepper powder: to taste

Butter: 1 tsp

METHOD

1. Wash the drumsticks. Run a knife through the centre so it splits open. Scoop out the pulp and set aside. Peel and chop the bottle gourd into big pieces.

2. Heat oil in a pressure cooker. Add ginger and sauté until brown. Add the drumsticks, bottle gourd pieces, water, pepper powder and salt. Cook for 3 whistles.

3. Blend the cooked vegetables and make a puree. Strain the puree and transfer to a pan. Heat and stir well. Add butter. Sprinkle some pepper powder before serving.

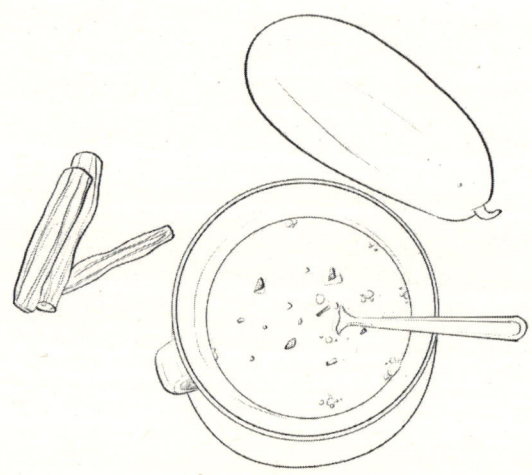

Jams, Pickles, Chutneys and Chutney Powders

JAMS

1. Banana Jam
2. Apple and Banana Jam
3. Pineapple Jam

PICKLES

1. How to Preserve Raw Mangoes in Brine
2. Tender Mango Pickle
3. Kadu Manga (Special Mango Pickle)
4. Minced Mango Pickle
5. Mango Pickle 1
6. Mango Pickle 2
7. Chiranjeevi Pickle
8. Lime Pickle 1
9. Lime Pickle 2
10. Sweet Pickle with Lime
11. Lime Raisin Pickle
12. Chinese Orange Date Pickle
13. Pineapple Sweet Pickle
14. Brinjal Pickle
15. Mixed Vegetable Pickle
16. Fish Pickle

CHUTNEYS AND CHUTNEY POWDERS

1. Ginger Curry
2. Pickled Mango Chutney (Uppumanga Chammanthi)
3. Chutney for Boiled Tapioca
4. Mulaku Chutta Chammanthi
5. Coconut Chutney
6. Mango and Coconut Chutney
7. Coconut and Dry Red Chilli Chutney
8. Dried Fish and Coconut Chutney
9. Roasted Coconut Chutney
10. Tomato Chutney
11. Chutney Powder or 'Gun' Powder
12. Coconut Chutney Powder
13. Curry Leaves Powder
14. Prawn Powder

Jams

1. Banana Jam

A traditional recipe that uses a particular variety of banana, the palayankodan.

Yields: 3 bottles of 1 l each

INGREDIENTS

Bananas (palayankodan variety): 3 kg

Water: 2 l

Black grapes: ¼ kg

Water: ½ l

Sugar: 1 kg

Cinnamon: 4

Cloves: 10

METHOD

1. Remove the skin and cut the bananas into small pieces. Cook them in water till soft, and make a puree. Strain and squeeze the puree through a muslin cloth and set aside.

2. Wash the grapes and cook in water. Strain the grape pulp through a sieve.

3. Take a heavy-bottomed pan and mix both the purees. Add sugar, cinnamon and cloves. Cook on high flame till it starts boiling.

4. Keep removing the thick greyish residue (banana starch) that will appear on top. Reduce flame and let it simmer. Cook until the jam is thick.

5. To test the consistency of the jam, put a drop in a saucer containing water. If the jam does not spread into the water, it is done.

6. Pour the warm jam into sterilized glass bottles. Close the lids once it is completely cool.

2. Apple and Banana Jam

Ginger adds a kick to this jam which combines apples and bananas.

Yields: 1 bottle of 1 l

INGREDIENTS

Apples: ¼ kg

Robusta bananas: ½ kg

Sugar: Slightly less than 850 g

Juice of 1 lime

Ginger, coarsely ground:
1-inch piece

METHOD

1. Peel the apples and bananas, and cut them into pieces. In a pressure cooker, add enough water to cover the fruits. Add lime juice and the coarsely ground ginger. Pressure cook for 20 minutes.

2. Open the pressure cooker and add sugar. Cook on a high flame for the first 10 minutes. Then reduce the flame and allow to simmer till the mixture gets a semi-solid consistency.

3. To test, pour a little jam into a saucer containing water. If it spreads, it needs to be cooked for some more time. If it does not, then the jam is ready.

4. Pour the warm jam into sterilized glass bottles. Close the lids once it is completely cool.

3. Pineapple Jam

There's nothing quite like home-made pineapple jam; be sure to use only fresh, sweet pineapples.

Yields: 1 bottle of ½ l

INGREDIENTS

Pineapple, minced: 1 kg

Sugar: 750 g

Lime juice: 2 tbsp

Cloves: 5

METHOD

1. Add sugar and lime juice to the minced pineapple. Mix well and leave overnight in the refrigerator.

2. Transfer the pineapple to a heavy-bottomed vessel. Add cloves. Cook over a medium flame. Keep stirring and remove the scum as it appears on top.

3. When the jam reaches a single-thread consistency, remove from heat.

4. Store in clean, dry bottles once it cools.

Pickles

1. How to Preserve Raw Mangoes in Brine

If procured at the right time and preserved the right way, this can be the base for several pickles, chutneys or relishes.

Yields: 14 l

INGREDIENTS

Tender green mangoes: 6 kg

Salt: ½ kg

Water: 6 l

METHOD

1. Wash the mangoes well and wipe them dry.

2. Dissolve salt in water and boil it. Cool and strain.

3. Place the mangoes in a large, dry jar.

4. Stir the salt solution and pour it over the mangoes.

5. Store in a 10-litre jar.

6. Close the jar with an airtight lid and tie a soft cloth tightly around the lid. Preserve for two weeks before using the pickle.

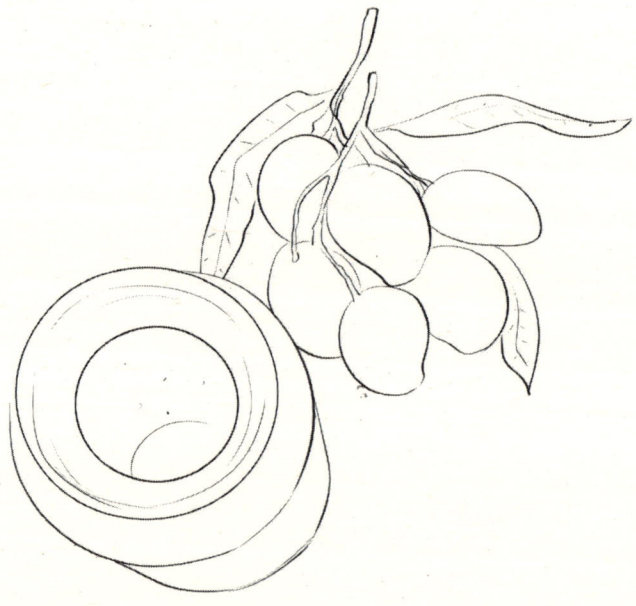

2. Tender Mango Pickle

Tender mango pickle is a favourite in most homes.

Yields: ¾ l

INGREDIENTS

Salted tender mangoes
(already preserved in brine):
1 kg

Chilli powder: ½ cup

Mustard seeds: ¼ cup

Asafoetida: ½ tsp

Gingelly oil: ½ cup

METHOD

1. Ladle 1½ cups of brine from the jar in which the mangoes are preserved into a bowl. Soak chilli powder in a few teaspoons of this mixture.

2. Powder mustard seeds and asafoetida after frying lightly in gingelly oil.

3. Mix the soaked chilli powder and powdered ingredients and grind to a paste. Add this to the salted mangoes.

4. Store in clean, dry bottles.

Note: The liquid should cover the mangoes. If more liquid is required, use the brine from the salted mangoes, adding more chilli powder to it, if necessary.

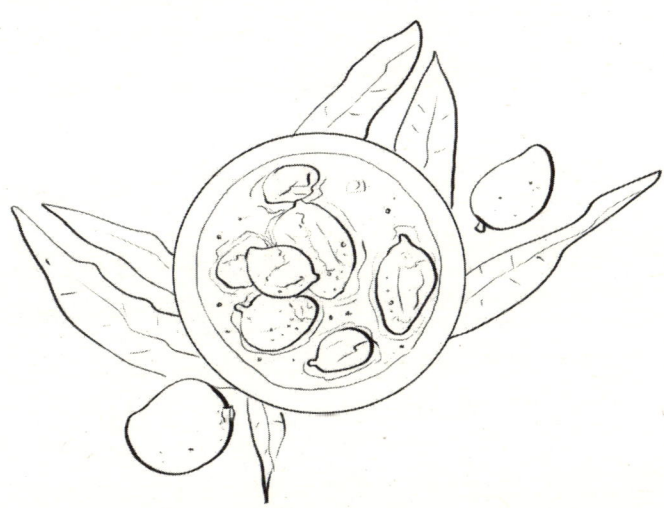

3. Kadu Manga (Special Mango Pickle)

This pickle can be made easily with just a few ingredients.

Yields: 1 l

INGREDIENTS

Raw mangoes: 1 kg

Salt: 6 tbsp

Chilli powder: 6 tbsp

Turmeric powder: 4 tsp

Mustard seeds: 2 tsp

Fenugreek seeds: 2 tsp

Ginger, sliced into thin pcs: 4 tbsp

Garlic cloves: 4 tbsp

Gingelly oil: 1 cup

Asafoetida powder: 4 tsp

Sugar: 2 tsp

Curry leaves: A handful

METHOD

1. Peel the mangoes and cut into small even pieces. Coat the pieces with salt and marinate for 2 hours.

2. Heat a wok and add oil. Splutter mustard seeds, fenugreek seeds and curry leaves. Add ginger and garlic and sauté.

3. Lower the flame and add chilli, turmeric and asafoetida powders. Sauté again.

4. Add the mango pieces and sugar. Mix well. Remove from flame.

5. Allow the pickle to cool before bottling.

4. Minced Mango Pickle

Minced mango gives this pickle a unique texture.

Yields: 400 g

INGREDIENTS

Raw mangoes, peeled and very finely chopped: 4 cups

Gingelly oil: 1 cup

Salt to taste

Turmeric powder: 1 tsp

Chilli powder: 1 tbsp

Fenugreek seeds, roasted and powdered: ½ tsp

Asafoetida, roasted and powdered: ½ tsp

METHOD

1. Heat 2 tbsp oil in a wok. Sauté the minced mangoes lightly. Add salt, turmeric and chilli powders and stir well.

2. Before removing from the flame, sprinkle fenugreek and asafoetida powders and mix well.

3. Heat the leftover oil and let it cool. Pour on top of the pickle. There should always be a thin layer of oil on top.

4. Store the pickle in glass bottles with tight-fitting lids.

5. Mango Pickle 1

This recipe and the one that follows are just two examples of the several regional and local variations for mango pickles.

Yields: 750 g

INGREDIENTS

Mangoes: 1 kg

Salt to taste

Gingelly oil: ¾ cup

Fenugreek seeds: 1 tsp

Mustard seeds: 1 tsp

Vinegar: 1 cup

Garlic paste, ground with vinegar: 2 tbsp

Ginger paste, ground with vinegar: 1 tbsp

Chilli powder: ½ cup to ¾ cup

Asafoetida powder: 1 tbsp

Sugar: 2 tsp

Salt to taste

METHOD

1. Wash and wipe the mangoes dry. Slice them with the skin into finger-like pieces. Apply salt and set aside for 1 hour.

2. Heat a wok and pour in some oil. Splutter mustard and fenugreek seeds. Add garlic and ginger pastes and sauté well. Once oil clears on the surface, remove from heat and add chilli powder. Mix well.

3. Add vinegar and mix the rest of the gravy from the salted mangoes. Put the wok back on low flame. Stir well till the gravy thickens.

4. Add asafoetida powder and sugar. Continue stirring and adjust the sugar and salt.

5. Finally, add mangoes and mix well.

6. Once cold, store in airtight bottles. Make sure there is a layer of oil on top.

6. Mango Pickle 2

Yields: 3 kg

INGREDIENTS

Raw mangoes: 25

Salt to taste

Chilli powder: 2½ cups

Turmeric powder: ½ cup

Fenugreek seeds: 6½ tbsp

Husked mustard seeds: 1½ cups

Garlic cloves: 1½ cups

Vinegar: 1 cup or more

Gingelly oil: 3 cups

METHOD

1. Wash and wipe the mangoes dry. Slice into finger-like pieces. Apply salt and keep aside for one and a half days. Separate the mango pieces from the salted liquid (brine).

2. Grind chilli powder, turmeric powder, fenugreek seeds, husked mustard seeds and garlic with the brine. Add vinegar if required.

3. Heat gingelly oil in a heavy-bottomed wok. On a low flame, sauté the ground ingredients and fry till the oil surfaces on top.

4. Remove from heat and add the sliced mangoes. Mix well. Check salt and vinegar.

5. Store the pickle in airtight bottles. Make sure there is enough oil on top.

7. Chiranjeevi Pickle

The addition of husked mustard seeds gives this recipe a different flavour altogether.

Yields: 2 kg

INGREDIENTS

Mangoes: 3 kg

Chilli powder: 1½ cups

Salt to taste

Mustard seeds, husked: 1½ cups

Dry ginger powder: 1 tbsp

Fenugreek seeds, roasted and powdered: 1 tbsp

Pepper powder: ½ tbsp

Turmeric powder: ½ tbsp

Cloves: 24

For tempering

Gingelly oil: 1½ cups

Mustard seeds: 1 tbsp

Garlic cloves: 1 cup

Ginger, sliced: ½ cup

Asafoetida powder: 1 tbsp

Chilli powder: ½ cup

Vinegar: 2 cups

Salt to taste

Sugar: 6 tbsp

METHOD

1. Cut the mangoes into half and remove the seed and thread-like portion with a knife. Chop into medium-sized pieces.

2. Marinate the pieces with salt. Keep it covered in a steel vessel for 3 days.

3. In a bowl, mix all the ingredients listed from chilli powder to cloves. Coat the mangoes with these ingredients and keep in an airtight jar for 10 days. Stir the ingredients well once a while with a clean, dry spoon.

4. On the 10th day, separate the mango pieces from the gravy and keep the pieces out in the sun again for 3 days. After that, mix the mangoes with the gravy and set aside.

5. Heat oil in a heavy-bottomed vessel and splutter mustard seeds, garlic cloves and ginger.

6. Lower the flame and add chilli and asafoetida powders. Sauté and finally add the mango pieces, along with vinegar and sugar. Mix everything well. Remove from flame and add salt to taste. Allow the pickle to cool. Store in airtight bottles.

8. Lime Pickle 1

As with mango, lime pickles too have many variations.

Yields: 2 kg

INGREDIENTS

Limes: 25

Gingelly oil: ½ cup

Mustard seeds: 2 tsp

Fenugreek seeds: 1 tsp

Turmeric powder: 1 tsp

Garlic cloves: ½ cup

Ginger, julienned: 2 tbsp

Green chillies, slit: 18

Asafoetida powder: 1 tsp

Chilli powder: 2 tbsp

Salt: ¾ cup

METHOD

1. Steam the limes for 5 minutes. Spread on a tray to cool and wipe dry.

2. Heat oil, splutter mustard seeds and add fenugreek seeds. Lower the flame and add turmeric powder.

3. Add garlic, ginger and green chillies, and sauté till the colour changes to a very pale brown.

4. Remove from flame and add asafoetida and chilli powders. Mix well and when cool, add salt.

5. Cut each lime into 8 pieces. Place the pieces in a clean and dry jar, alternating each layer with a layer of the sautéed ingredients. Use after 1 week.

9. Lime Pickle 2

Yields: 1.2 kg

INGREDIENTS

Limes: 1 kg

Salt: ¼ cup

Gingelly oil: ¼ cup

Mustard seeds: 1 tsp

Fenugreek seeds: ¼ tsp

Mixed green and red chillies
(ripe), half slit: 18

Ginger slices: 1 tbsp

Garlic cloves: ½ cup

Water: 1 cup

Vinegar: ¼ cup

Sugar: 1 tsp

Salt to taste

METHOD

1. Wash and wipe the limes. Steam till soft. Do not allow them to split. Remove and wipe away the moisture.

2. Cut the limes into quarters. Mix ¼ cup salt and keep for 2 days to soften.

3. Heat a heavy-bottomed skillet. Splutter mustard seeds and fenugreek seeds. Sauté green and red chillies, ginger and garlic. Remove from flame and when cool, add to the salted limes.

4. Boil water, vinegar, sugar and salt in a pan. Once it cools, pour into the pickle.

5. Store in airtight bottles.

10. Sweet Pickle with Lime

Sweet pickles are excellent as relishes, as an accompaniment to biryanis and pulaos and even to flavour meat.

Yields: 200 g

INGREDIENTS

Limes: 10

Ajwain (caraway seeds): 1 tsp

Turmeric powder: 1 tsp

Red chilli powder: 2 tsp or more according to taste

Salt: 4–5 tsp

Sugar: 1 cup

METHOD

1. Wash the limes and wipe them dry. Cut into quarter-inch pieces. Add ajwain, turmeric powder, red chilli powder and salt. Mix thoroughly, and store in an airtight jar. Leave in the sun for 1 week. Stir the contents of the jar with a dry spoon a couple of times during the week.

2. After a week, when the limes turn soft, add 1 cup sugar. Continue keeping the jar in the sun and stirring with a dry spoon a couple of times a week until you see that the sugar has dissolved completely and coated the lime pieces like a syrup. This will take a week. Finally, grind the lime mixture to a fine paste in a mixer. It will look like a preserve. Store in airtight bottles. Best served with biryani or pulao.

11. Lime Raisin Pickle

This sweet and sour pickle is everyone's favourite.

Yields: 3 kg

INGREDIENTS

Limes: 50

Salt: 1 cup

Sugar: 2 cups

Vinegar: ½ cup

Raisins: 2 cups

Chilli powder: ½–¾ cup

Mustard seeds: ½ tsp

Fenugreek seeds: ½ tsp

Garlic cloves, sliced thin: ½ tbsp

Ginger, sliced thin: 2 tsp

Gingelly oil: 1½ cups

Dry red chillies, cut into 3 pcs after removing the seeds: 1 cup

Garlic cloves: 1 cup

Ginger: ½ cup

Mustard seeds: 2 tbsp

Fenugreek seeds: 2 tbsp

Powdered cumin: ½ tsp

METHOD

1. Steam the limes till they are soft. Dry and cut them into 8 pieces without breaking them apart. Add sugar and salt and keep them in the sun for 2 days.

2. Grind raisins, chilli powder, mustard seeds, fenugreek seeds, garlic and ginger into a paste using vinegar.

3. Heat some oil in a wok and sauté the dry red chillies, garlic cloves and ginger, then remove them from the wok. Add the rest of the oil, splutter mustard seeds and fenugreek seeds and the ground paste. Fry well till the oil floats on top. Sprinkle some cumin powder. Mix everything together and cool.

4. Stuff the ground ingredients into each lime (just enough so you can close the lime to some extent) and leave the rest to coat the limes. Store in airtight bottles.

12. Chinese Orange Date Pickle

The tart sweetness of oranges and the richness of dates come together in this pickle.

Yields: 500 g

INGREDIENTS

Chinese oranges: 25

Salt: 3 heaped tbsp

Vinegar: 1 cup

Dates, chopped: 1 cup

Ginger and garlic, julienned:
1 tbsp each

Ginger and garlic, made into
paste: 1 tbsp each

Chilli powder: 1 tbsp

Sugar: 1 cup

METHOD

1. Cut the oranges into halves. Add salt and store in a bottle for 10 days. Stir every once in a few days. On the 10th day, separate the oranges and discard the salt water.

2. Remove the seeds and slice the oranges into 4 pieces each. Chop the dates into small bits and set aside. Boil vinegar and leave it to cool.

3. Mix the ginger and garlic juliennes and paste, chilli powder and sugar with the vinegar. Finally, add the dates and oranges. Stir well. Store in airtight glass bottles.

13. Pineapple Sweet Pickle

This pickle is a tangy treat with a refreshing tropical flavour.

Yields: 250 g

INGREDIENTS

Mustard seeds: ½ tsp

Vinegar: 1 cup

Garlic cloves: 1 cup

Glacé cherries: 1 cup

Pineapple jam: 2 cups

Ginger paste: 1 tsp

Garlic paste: 1 tsp

Chilli powder: 1 tsp

Lime juice: ½ cup

Salt: ½ tsp

METHOD

1. Grind mustard seeds in vinegar. Set aside.

2. Steam the garlic cloves for about 2 minutes. Wipe them dry and set aside.

3. Cut the glacé cherries into halves and set aside.

4. Heat a heavy-bottomed saucepan. Add pineapple jam, glacé cherries, ginger and garlic pastes, lime juice, chilli powder, ground mustard, vinegar and salt.

5. Once the mixture starts bubbling, add the steamed garlic pods. Ensure that the pods don't break while mixing.

6. When the ingredients becomes thick, remove from flame and leave to cool.

14. Brinjal Pickle

A sweet and spicy pickle that goes well with almost all Indian dishes.

Yields: 250 g

INGREDIENTS

Brinjal: 500 g

Garlic: 3 tbsp

Ginger: 1 tbsp

Mustard seeds, roasted and powdered: ¾ tsp

Fenugreek seeds, roasted and powdered: ¾ tsp

Chilli powder: 2 tbsp

Turmeric powder: ½ tsp

Vinegar: ⅔ cup

Salt to taste

Sugar to taste

Oil for frying

METHOD

1. Slice the brinjal into 1-inch pieces. Marinate with salt and turmeric powder for 30 minutes. Rinse well and drain the brinjal pieces dry.

2. Grind garlic and ginger to a paste.

3. Heat oil in a wok. Half fry the brinjal pieces and remove from oil.

4. In the same oil, sauté the ground garlic and ginger. Fry well till oil appears on the top. Add chilli and turmeric powders and continue sautéing till the oil separates. Add mustard and fenugreek powders. Mix and sauté well.

5. Add the brinjal and cook till everything is well mixed, and the brinjal is fully cooked; this should take approximately 5 minutes. Finally add vinegar, salt and sugar.

6. Mix well and allow to cool before storing in airtight jars.

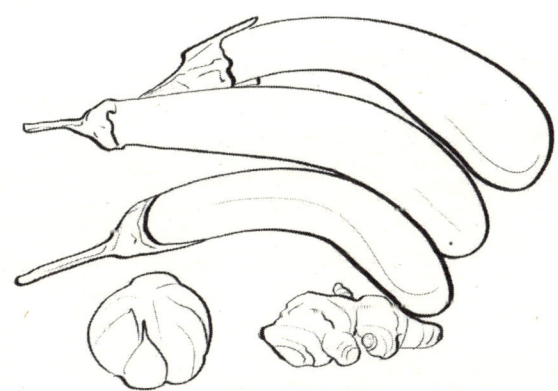

15. Mixed Vegetable Pickle

An unusual combination of vegetables makes this recipe different.

Yields: 350 g

INGREDIENTS

Carrot: 100 g

Bitter gourd: 100 g

Raw mango (not too sour): 100 g

Salt: 2 tbsp

Oil: ¼ cup

Mustard seeds: 1 tsp

Fenugreek seeds: 1 tsp

Turmeric powder: ½ tsp

Green chillies, slit: 10

Dry red chillies, broken into two: 4

Ginger, julienned : 2 tbsp

Garlic cloves, steamed: 100 g

Water: 1 cup

Lime juice: from 2 limes

Sugar: 1 tsp

Salt to taste

METHOD

1. Slice carrots, bitter gourd and mango into thin uniform pieces cut at a diagonal. Coat with 2 tbsp of salt and keep aside.

2. Heat oil in a wok. Splutter mustard seeds and add fenugreek seeds. Lower the flame and add turmeric powder followed by green chillies, dry red chillies and ginger. Sauté well and pour water.

3. Once the water starts to boil, add the steamed garlic cloves and the vegetables. Add sugar, lime juice and salt to taste. Mix well. Allow the pickle to cool.

4. Keep in airtight bottles. Store in the refrigerator.

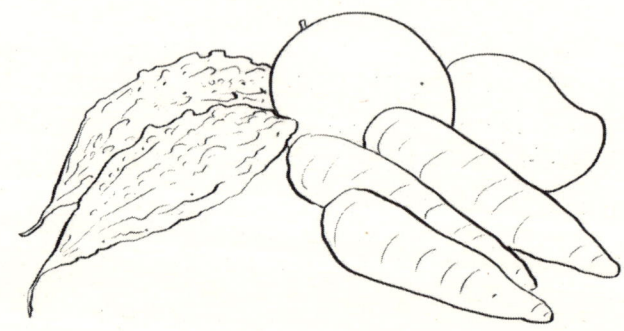

16. Fish Pickle

You could pickle any kind of fish, but boneless meaty pieces work best.

Yields: 1.5 kg

INGREDIENTS

Fish, cut into pcs: 1 kg

Pepper powder: 1 tsp

Turmeric powder: ¼ tsp

Oil: 1 cup

Onion, finely chopped: 2 cups

Garlic cloves: 2 tbsp

Ginger, finely sliced: 1 tbsp

Chilli powder: ½ cup

Mustard seeds: 1 tsp

Fenugreek seeds: ¾ tsp

Vinegar: ½ cup

Tomatoes, chopped: ½ cup

Water: 3 cups

Vinegar: ¼ cup

Sugar: 1 tsp

Salt to taste

METHOD

1. Wash and clean the fish pieces. Drain off the water completely. Marinate the pieces with pepper and turmeric powders and salt. Keep aside. Use ½ cup of vinegar and grind chilli powder, mustard seeds, fenugreek seeds, garlic and ginger.

2. Heat oil in a wok and lightly fry the fish pieces. Keep them aside.

3. Pour the rest of the oil and sauté onions until transparent. Add the ground ingredients and sauté again. Add tomatoes and fry till the oil separates. Add water. Mix well and allow to boil. Add vinegar, sugar and salt into the boiling gravy.

4. Remove from flame. Allow the gravy to cool a bit and then add the fried fish pieces while the gravy is still warm. Mix well.

5. The fish pieces should be immersed in the gravy and there should be a layer of oil on top. Once it cools, store in airtight bottles.

Chutneys and Chutney Powders

1. Ginger Curry

This is a staple for the Onam sadya and also serves as a relish.

Yields: 200 g

INGREDIENTS

Oil: ¼ cup

Mustard seeds: ½ tsp

Dry red chillies, halved: 3

Curry leaves: 3 sprigs

Ginger cubes, cut into 1-inch pcs: 6

Coconut bits, finely cut: 1 tbsp

Shallots, cut into thin slices: ¼ cup

Green chillies, cut in rounds: 5

Chilli powder: 1 tbsp

Turmeric powder: ¼ tsp

Asafoetida powder: ¼ tsp

Tamarind, the size of a lime, soaked in water: 1 cup

Jaggery, grated: 1 tsp

Salt to taste

METHOD

1. Crush ginger and squeeze out the juice. Chop ginger into very small bits and fry them in ¼ cup oil. Remove and grind coarsely. Set aside.

2. In the same oil, fry coconut bits and set aside. Using the same oil, splutter mustard seeds and add dry red chillies, shallots, green chillies and curry leaves.

3. Add chilli, turmeric and asafoetida powders. Again, cook on a low flame and fry lightly till the raw smell disappears. Add ginger and coconut bits. Add tamarind extract. Mix well. Simmer on a low flame.

4. Lastly, add jaggery. Let it simmer until the jaggery melts. Remove from flame.

5. Once cool, store in airtight bottles. This chutney cannot be kept for more than 4 days.

2. Pickled Mango Chutney (Uppumanga Chammanthi)

Chutneys like this one perk up even the blandest dishes.

Yields: 250 g

INGREDIENTS

Mango, pickled in brine and slightly crushed: 1 cup

Shallots, cut into rounds: 12

Green chillies, cut into rounds: 2

Curry leaves: 2 sprigs

Coconut milk, thick: 1 cup

Grated coconut: ¼ cup

Salt to taste

Coconut oil: 1 tsp

Mustard seeds: ¼

Dry red chillies broken into two: 2

Curry leaves: 2 sprigs

METHOD

1. Crush shallots, green chillies, grated coconut and curry leaves and mix with the mango pieces. Add coconut milk and salt to taste.

2. Heat oil in a wok and splutter mustard seeds. Add dry red chillies and curry leaves. Sauté and pour over the curry.

3. Chutney for Boiled Tapioca

This is a staple in most Malayali households.

Yields: 150 g

INGREDIENTS

Shallots: 6

Green chillies: 4

Curry leaves: 1 sprig

Curd (not too sour): 1 cup

Coconut oil: 1 tsp

Salt to taste

METHOD

1. In a mixer, crush shallots, green chillies and curry leaves lightly.

2. Mix the crushed ingredients with curd and add salt to taste.

3. Lastly, add coconut oil. Mix well. Serve.

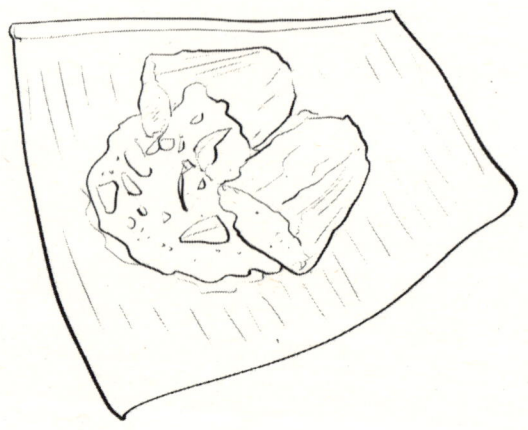

4. Mulaku Chutta Chammanthi

Tamarind and fried or roasted chillies add an exciting flavour to this variant.

Yields: 150 g

INGREDIENTS

Dry red chillies: 12

Shallots: 15

Curry leaves: 1 sprig

Tamarind: 1 (size of a marble)

Salt to taste

Coconut oil for frying and garnish

METHOD

1. Fry the dry red chillies in hot coconut oil. Do not use this oil again. You could also roast the chillies over an open flame.

2. Crush the fried chillies with shallots and curry leaves in a mixie or with a mortar and pestle.

3. Extract the juice from the tamarind and add to the crushed items. Add salt to taste.

4. Pour some fresh coconut oil over the chutney. Mix well.

5. You can use this chutney for 2–4 days if stored in a glass container.

5. Coconut Chutney

This is the most common version, used as an accompaniment to idlis, dosas and vadas.

Yields: 200 g

INGREDIENTS

Grated coconut: 1½ cups

Shallots, cut into bits: 2

Ginger, sliced: 1-inch piece

Green chillies, sliced: 2

Roasted gram dal: 1 tbsp (optional)

Salt to taste

Oil: 2 tbsp

Mustard seeds: ½ tsp

Shallots, sliced: 4

Dry red chillies, halved: 2

Curry leaves: 1 sprig

METHOD

1. Coarsely grind grated coconut, shallots, ginger, green chillies and roasted gram dal in a mixie. Use ¼ cup water to get a loose consistency. Add salt to taste.

To season

1. Heat oil in a wok. Splutter mustard seeds. Add shallots, dry red chillies and curry leaves. Sauté well and pour over the chutney.

6. Mango and Coconut Chutney

This variant of the coconut chutney is a favourite among all age groups.

Yields: 200 g

INGREDIENTS

Grated coconut: 1½ cups

Shallots, sliced: 2

Ginger, sliced: 1-inch piece

Green chillies, sliced: 2

Curry leaves: 1 sprig

Raw mango: 1 big slice

Salt to taste

METHOD

1. In a mixie, add coconut, shallots, ginger, green chillies, curry leaves and mango slice. Grind them well and add salt to taste. While serving, gather the ingredients together and make a neat, compact ball.

7. Coconut and Dry Red Chilli Chutney

A classic chutney to add a spicy accompaniment to a variety of dishes.

Yields: 200 g

INGREDIENTS

Grated coconut: 1½ cups

Shallots: 2

Ginger: 1-inch pc

Dry red chillies: 2

Salt to taste

Water: ¼ cup

Oil: 1 tbsp

Mustard seeds: ½ tsp

Shallots, sliced: 2

Curry leaves: 1 sprig

Dry red chillies: 2

METHOD

1. In a mixie, add coconut, shallots, ginger, dry red chillies and salt. Grind into a coarse paste. Add water and mix well.

2. In a heavy-bottomed pan or wok, heat oil. Splutter mustard seeds, add shallots, dry red chillies and curry leaves and sauté well. Remove from flame and stir into the chutney. Serve.

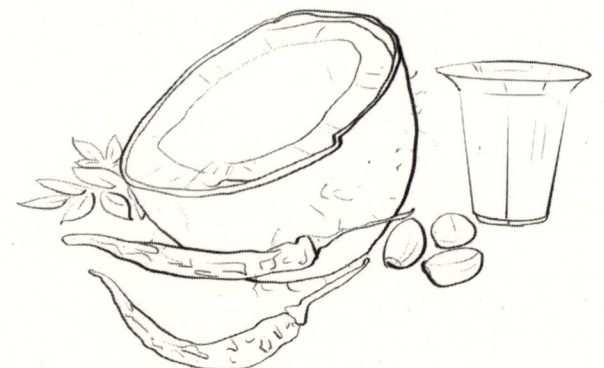

8. Dried Fish and Coconut Chutney

This one is best paired with rice and is relished by all Malayalis.

Yields: 350 g

INGREDIENTS

Dried fish: 1 cup

Grated coconut: 2 cups

Shallots: 4

Curry leaves: 1 sprig

Dry red chillies: 4

Oil: 1 tbsp

METHOD

1. Soak the dried fish in water for 10 minutes. Rinse well and pat dry.

2. In a small wok or skillet, heat oil. Add the washed, dried fish and sauté lightly. Remove and debone if needed. Pound the fish using a mortar and pestle.

3. In the same wok, dry roast coconut and when it is half done, add dry red chillies. Continue roasting until the coconut is golden brown in colour.

4. Grind shallots and curry leaves in a mixie. Add the powdered fish and roasted coconut. Continue grinding till the chutney takes on the texture of coarse breadcrumbs.

5. Transfer to a serving bowl. Serve.

9. Roasted Coconut Chutney

This one is a delicious and traditional accompaniment to kanji and payar, but can be enjoyed with dosas too.

Yields: 250 g

INGREDIENTS

Grated coconut: 2 cups

Dry red chillies: 4

Shallots: 3

Ginger slices: 1 tsp

Curry leaves: 3 sprigs

Salt to taste

Tamarind as required

METHOD

1. Roast the grated coconut and dry red chillies. Grind these together with the remaining ingredients to make the chutney.

10. Tomato Chutney

Tomato chutneys can be made in many different ways; this recipe is a favourite for dosas and idlis.

Yields: 100 g

INGREDIENTS

Oil: 1 tbsp

Onion, finely minced: 1 big

Ginger, finely minced: 1-inch piece

Garlic cloves, minced: 4

Chilli powder: ½ tsp

Turmeric powder: A pinch

Tomatoes, finely minced: 4

Salt to taste

Sugar: 1 pinch

METHOD

1. Heat oil in a wok. Add minced onion, ginger and garlic. Stir till the onions are transparent. Add chilli and turmeric powders. Add tomatoes, stir, and continue sautéing till a thick gravy is formed. Add salt to taste.

2. If the tomatoes are sour, add a little sugar.

11. Chutney Powder or 'Gun' Powder

A combination of dals, parboiled rice and dry red chillies, roasted and powdered together, creates this spicy chutney powder usually served with dosas and idlis.

Yields: 400 g

INGREDIENTS

Gingelly oil: 1 tsp

Dry red chillies: 30

Parboiled rice: ¾ cup

Asafoetida powder: 2 tsp

Husked black beans: 5 tbsp

Split green gram: 5 tbsp

Bengal gram: 5 tbsp

Salt to taste

METHOD

1. Heat oil in a heavy-bottomed skillet and sauté all the ingredients except salt. Powder them coarsely, add salt and use as chutney powder.

2. It is usually served mixed with refined coconut or gingelly oil.

12. Coconut Chutney Powder

This chutney powder tastes best when made with freshly grated coconut, slowly roasted to a rich dark brown. In my mother's kitchen, it was then pounded the old-fashioned way, with shallots and spices into a delicious mix.

Yields: 250 g

INGREDIENTS

Coconut, grated: 6 cups

Shallots, chopped: 6

Ginger, finely chopped: 1 tbsp

Curry leaves: 10 sprigs

Dry red chillies: 15

Coriander seeds: 1 tsp

Peppercorns: 1 tsp

Tamarind, gooseberry-sized ball: 1

Salt: 1 tsp

METHOD

1. In a large heavy-bottomed pan or wok, roast the grated coconut, shallots, ginger, curry leaves, dry red chillies, coriander seeds and peppercorns. Roast until the coconut is brown in colour. Add the remaining ingredients and grind coarsely.

2. Continue grinding till the chutney takes on the texture of coarse breadcrumbs. Cool well and bottle it.

13. Curry Leaves Powder

Yields: 100 g

INGREDIENTS

Oil: 1 tbsp

Curry leaves: 1 cup

Dry red chillies: 4

Garlic: 3

Coconut, grated: 1 tbsp

Bengal gram: 1 tbsp

Black chickpeas: 1 tbsp

Sesame seeds: 1 tbsp

Cumin seeds: 1 tsp

Salt to taste

METHOD

1. Wash and dry the curry leaves.

2. Heat oil in a skillet and fry the leaves till they are crisp. Remove from flame.

3. Dry roast red chillies, garlic, grated coconut, sesame seeds, Bengal gram, black chickpeas and cumin seeds. Add all the ingredients into a mixie along with the fried curry leaves and salt to taste. Grind coarsely, powder and store in airtight bottles.

14. Prawn Powder

This can be mixed with hot rice and a dollop of ghee.

Yields: 250 g

INGREDIENTS

Coconut oil: 2 tbsp

Mustard seeds: 1 tsp

Dry red chillies: 2

Curry leaves: 2 sprigs

Shallots, finely chopped:
1 heaped cup

½ a coconut, grated

Chilli powder: 1 tsp

Garlic cloves: 3

Turmeric powder: ¼ tsp

Dried shrimp, roasted and
ground: 150 g

Salt to taste

METHOD

1. Heat coconut oil and splutter mustard seeds. Sauté dry red chillies and curry leaves. Add shallots and sauté well.

2. Mix coconut, chilli powder and garlic cloves together. Crush coarsely. Add turmeric powder and mix with the sautéed ingredients. Fry well on a low flame.

3. Add shrimp powder and salt to taste. Mix well and remove from flame. Store in airtight bottles.

Glossary

Bengal Gram	Kadala Parippu	Chana Dal
Red Cowpeas	Van Payar	Lobiya
Gram Flour	Kadala Maavu	Besan
Husked Black Beans	Uzhunnu Parippu	Urad Dal
Split Green Gram	Cherupayar Parippu	Moong Dal
Pigeon Peas	Tuvara Parippu	Toor Dal
Black Chickpeas	Kadala	Chana
Asafoetida	Kaayam	Hing
Button Onion/Shallot	Chuvannulli	Chota Pyaz
Onion	Savaala	Pyaz
Kokum	Kudampuli	Kokum
Tamarind	Vaalanpuli	Imli
Coconut	Thenga	Naariyal
Coconut Milk	Thengappal	Naariyal ka Dhoodh
Curry Leaves	Curryveppila	Curry Patta
Ghee	Ney	Makhan
Curd	Thairu	Dahi
Cinnamon	Karuvapatta	Dalchini
Clove	Graambu	Laung
Cardamom	Elakkai	Elaichi
Ginger	Inchi	Adrak
Garlic	Veluthulli	Lahsun

Green Chilli . . . . Pachamulak . . . . Hari Mirch

Dry Red Chilli . . . . Vattal Mulak . . . . Lal Mirch

Coriander. . . . . Malli . . . . Dhaniya

Turmeric Powder . . . . Manjal Podi . . . . Haldi

Peppercorn . . . . Kurumulak . . . . Kaali Mirch

Cumin Seed . . . . Jeerakam . . . . Jeera

Aniseed. . . . . Perumjeerakam . . . . Saunf

Fenugreek Seeds . . . . Uluva . . . . Methi

Sesame Seeds . . . . Ellu . . . . Til

Refined Flour . . . . Maida . . . . Maida

Wheat Flour . . . . Gothambu Podi . . . . Aatta

Semolina . . . . Rava . . . . Sooji

Rice Flakes . . . . Aval . . . . Chaaval ke Ghuchche

Rice Flour . . . . Arippodi . . . . Chaaval ka Aatta

Jaggery . . . . Sharkkara . . . . Gur

Dried Ginger . . . . Chukku . . . . Sookhe Adrak

Tapioca . . . . Kappa . . . .

Bay Leaf . . . . Vazhana Ila . . . . Tej Patta